I0762547

SUNDAY DINNER
with NONNA GRACIE

SUNDAY DINNER *with* NONNA GRACIE

Traditional Italian Recipes for Gathering and Sharing

GRACE GERAMITA

with MATT GRESIA

Publisher Mike Sanders
Art & Design Director William Thomas
Editorial Director Ann Barton
Senior Editor Brook Farling
Designer Rebecca Batchelor
Developmental Editor Tiffany Taing
Copy Editor Christy Wagner
Food Photographer Daniel Showalter
Food and Prop Stylist Lovoni Walker
Chef Ashley Brooks
Lifestyle Photographers Garrett Bruce, Christian Flamio
Recipe Tester Thom England
Proofreaders Jean Bissell, Jennifer Weltich
Indexer Michael Goldstein

First American Edition, 2026
Published in the United States by DK Publishing
1745 Broadway, 20th Floor, New York, NY 10019

The authorized representative in the EEA is Dorling Kindersley Verlag GmbH. Arnulfstr. 124, 80636 Munich, Germany

26 26 27 28 30 10 9 8 7 6 5 4 3 2 1
001-351405-APR2026

A catalog record for this book is available from the Library of Congress.
ISBN 979-8-2171-2812-9

DK books are available at special discounts when purchased in bulk for sales promotions, premiums, fund-raising, or educational use. For details, contact SpecialSales@dk.com

Printed and bound in China

www.dk.com

This book was made with Forest Stewardship Council™ certified paper – one small step in DK's commitment to a sustainable future.
Learn more at
www.dk.com/uk/information/sustainability

To my beloved husband, John. You had big dreams, and although you left us long ago, your love and hopes have stayed with me all these years. Back then, you never would have believed that I would go on to write a cookbook, let alone work with one of the biggest publishing companies around. This book is dedicated to you and your dream of being an author. It is as much yours as it is mine, and I hope I've made you proud. I love you.

Contents

Foreword

by Mark Iacono

Founder of Lucali, New York City's most iconic pizza restaurant

Few memories are quite as vivid as waking up to the old Sunday morning alarm clock: the sounds of pots clanging in the kitchen, accompanied by the incredible scent of garlic browning in the sauce pot. From three floors down, that noise and smell would reach me before my feet hit the floor. That's how I knew it was Sunday. And in my house, Sunday meant one thing: family. You didn't need a calendar. You didn't need an invitation. You just knew what was in store. Waking up every Sunday felt like waking up on Christmas morning. But it wasn't about the toys. The excitement came from the people I would soon be spending time with.

Now, don't get me wrong—the food was always great. But growing up, it was never really about the food. It was about the table. It was about who was sitting at that table. My great-aunts, great-uncles, cousins, neighbors, or whoever happened to show up. The more people, the better. That's how I always felt as a kid. And that table just kept getting longer. My uncle worked for a furniture company, and I still remember the day he had this massive custom table delivered just to fit everyone. We still ran out of space sometimes.

My grandmother was the center of it all. She didn't have a big arsenal of recipes, and she didn't use fancy ingredients. She certainly wasn't the type of cook who could throw together a million different dishes. In fact, she learned how to cook her few signature dishes from her clients in her basement beauty parlor. But the few things she did make? They were unforgettable. Her sauce is a great example—people talk about tomatoes like they have to be imported from Italy and hand-squeezed by monks. Nope. My grandmother made some of the best sauce I've ever had. I remember one time, in a pinch, she used Del Monte canned tomatoes. And you know what? It was sick. It was beautiful. Because it wasn't about the ingredients—it was about the hands that made it, the love behind it, and the people it brought together.

When we were young, my grandmother let us be part of her cooking. I remember sitting at the table with her, picking parsley leaves off the stems. We kids would stick the stems in our mouths and pretend they were straws of hay, like little old farmers. And the black olives? Forget it. She'd stick one on each of our fingers, and we'd eat them off like it was a game. The kitchen wasn't a place to stay out of—it was a place to grow up in.

We weren't eating filet mignon. We were eating pasta, meat, and salad—that's it. And lots of bread, of course. At the time, we kids made a big deal out of Sunday dinners. I remember the competitions we used to have of who could pile the most pasta on their plate and who could finish the biggest dish. Everyone had their preferences, too—flat dish, deep bowl, extra sauce, light sauce. And the rules were unwritten but understood: Don't take someone else's spot, don't criticize the food unless you're ready to hear it back, and never—ever—miss a Sunday dinner without a damn good reason.

At the end of those Sunday nights, you could see the exhaustion in my grandmother—even though she never let you know about it. She never complained, never asked for help, but you could see it in the way she eased into a chair after the table cleared. If it wasn't me, someone would always walk up behind her and give her a shoulder rub. She never turned it down. That was our quiet way of saying thank you. Of letting her know we appreciated her. And that little gesture—it meant everything.

I didn't move out of the house until I was 35. Not because I couldn't—because I didn't want to. I knew my grandmother wasn't going to be around forever, and I wasn't going to waste that time. Eventually, when I did move out, I would leave work and instead of going to my apartment, I'd go straight to her. Just to sit, just to eat, just to be near her. Spending so much time with her wasn't an obligation—it was a privilege.

I lost my dad when I was 10, and my uncle passed away at a young age. My mother, my aunt, and my grandma raised us kids on their own, and that's when the table became even more sacred. It wasn't just Sunday anymore—it was every night, in the house we all lived in together. The dinner table became a place for healing, for laughter, for holding each other up. And let's not forget the discipline. With no men around, in addition to being mothers, the ladies were forced to play the role of father figures in our lives. During this time, I started to understand the weight of these dinners.

In those days, Carroll Gardens wasn't just a neighborhood in Brooklyn—it was a *community*. All of us kids were on the streets from morning until night. We'd play baseball in the park, even though it was entirely concrete, and when we weren't there, we were sitting on stoops, running between apartments, or just being kids. The neighborhood was alive in a way that's hard to find anymore. You had the local bakery, where the smell of fresh bread would hit you from a block away. The pork stores, where the owners knew not just your name, but also your family's order by heart. These weren't just businesses—they were extensions of everyone's kitchen, part of the fabric that held the whole place together. And the people behind them? They were our friends, and they cared about the neighborhood as much as we did. I remember Tony the butcher and the sawdust that covered his shop floor—as kids, that was our version of a modern-day foam party. I remember Tony standing behind the counter, peeking over my grandmother's shoulder with a smirk as I made snow angels in the sawdust behind her. He never said a word. He just watched, knowing exactly what was coming. He knew that if my grandmother turned around and caught me, there was a good chance I would catch the wooden spoon that sat inside her pocketbook. And yes—she really did carry it around for disciplinary purposes. Anyways, these absolute gems were littered across neighborhoods in all the five boroughs. Nowadays, it pains me to know that most people are missing out on that experience and instead are getting their groceries delivered from companies like FreshDirect and Instacart.

When I started Lucali, it wasn't about being a chef. I'm not a chef. I don't pretend to be. I'm not the guy creating crazy dishes and reinventing the wheel. Truthfully, I built Lucali because I missed what I grew up with. I missed Tony the butcher. I missed those burgundy-pinstripe enamel-paneled walls and the tin ceilings of his shop. The handwritten receipts written on torn brown paper bags. I even missed hating the pungent smell of the local baccalà store as a little kid. I longed for the overall feeling of my old neighborhood that was slowly becoming a different place. I couldn't bring the people back, but I could do my best to recreate that feeling.

People always ask me why Lucali doesn't have a massive menu, like the classic New York slice joints. The answer is simple: From day one, it was all about the pizza. I simply didn't need to introduce more dishes to the menu. Many pizzerias make garlic knots because they have leftover dough. Thankfully, I never had leftover dough to get rid of. If I was in a position where I had to, maybe I would have. That said, I'm happy it worked out this way. My skillset allows me to do a few things really well. That's how my grandmother was. That's how Nonna Gracie is. It's not about being a Michelin star chef. It's about the feeling of feeding people and seeing my pizza bring them joy. There's nothing more satisfying than watching peoples' first-time reactions from the pizza counter. For me, it's that look of disbelief. That I-didn't-think-it-was-possible-for-pizza-to-be-this-good look on their faces. That is what keeps me going.

Which brings me to Nonna.

One night at the restaurant, I was sitting out back with Nonna Gracie and her family. We were all around the table, eating, talking, laughing, and sharing similar stories of our pasts and our old neighborhoods. I reached over and grabbed Nonna's hand—and the moment I touched her skin, I choked up. Her knuckles were swollen, and her skin was soft but also worn from years of hard work. Holding her hand gave me a feeling I hadn't felt since my grandmother passed in 2001. It really felt like I was holding my grandmother's hand once again. I even had to take a photo of it, because I didn't want to forget what that moment gave me. That warmth. That connection. That grief and joy at the same time. It brought me right back to those Sunday nights when everyone else had gone home and it was just me and my grandmother sitting at the table, finishing off the bread, talking. That was always my favorite part of the evening.

When I watch Nonna Gracie, it takes me back to my own grandma. I see the same spark, the same warmth, the same command of a kitchen without needing to say much. She's not just cooking—she's creating a moment. She's bringing people in, holding them close, and saying, "Here, sit down with me, eat." And that means something.

She's preserving something that the world is starting to forget. She's keeping a way of life alive. You see her on the screen, and you remember your own grandmother, your own kitchen, your own spot at the table. That's why Nonna Gracie matters. Not just to her family, but to anyone who understands that cooking is love. That tradition matters. That it's not just about what's on the table, but who's around it. And unfortunately, those people aren't going to be around forever.

I've got one video, on DVD, of my grandmother. In it, she's making fresh pasta. That's it. That's all I have. Everything else lives in my head. I wish I had more. I wish I could hear her voice again. I wish I could watch her stir the sauce, her arthritic body hunched over the stove as she stretched to see inside the pot. I wish I could see her take a whiff of that pot and watch her eyes squint as she smiled, knowing she nailed it. The things I would do just to see again the way she passed a dish across the table. And that's what this cookbook gives people. It's not just recipes. It's not just food. It's memory. It's presence. It's a grandmother's love, frozen in time.

This book isn't just about Nonna Gracie. It's about what she represents. It's about family. About showing up. About keeping the thread from unraveling. It's about understanding that one day, your people won't be around. But the meals you make, the stories you pass down, the traditions you hold onto—that's how they live on. That's why we stay at the table, even after the chair is empty.

And somehow, we always bounce back. The chairs left empty are soon occupied again as the family grows. The baton gets passed—maybe quietly, maybe without anyone even realizing it—and the next generation starts hosting the Sunday dinners. The family members we once looked up to become memories, and we become the ones telling the stories. I used to be the kid listening to my uncles go on about the old days. Now I'm one of them telling the stories. And some day, someone will say, "Remember when Uncle Mark told us about that time a blue crab stole Gram's cigarette?" Eventually, it will be my daughter, nieces, and nephews who take over the tradition. And that's what makes it so special. That's what keeps it going. When Grandma isn't around anymore, someone will step in and try to fill her shoes.

But filling those shoes entirely is a near-impossible task. No one will ever touch your heart in the same way a grandmother does. It's a special kind of love that goes both ways. If you're lucky enough to still have your grandmother, hold her hand. Ask her questions. Listen to her stories. Pick parsley with her. Eat the olives she placed on your fingers. If you don't, use this book. Let it take you home. Let it sit with you like a Sunday sauce simmering on the stove all day. Let it feed you—not just your stomach, but also your heart.

Because when it's all said and done, the only thing that really matters is who you break bread with.

—Mark Iacono
Founder, Lucali

P.S. Now go call your grandmother.

Introduction

From my heart to yours, I welcome you into my kitchen, where every meal is a lesson, and every recipe is a memory. Writing this book has been a dream come true, but it's also a journey—one I never expected to take. As I sit here today, sharing these pages with you, I'm reminded of all the years I've spent in the kitchen with my family, cooking the dishes that have been passed down through generations. Each meal I make is a way of showing love, and every dish holds a little piece of my heart. It's been an incredible ride, and I'm so grateful to share it with all of you now.

When I first came to this country, I didn't speak a word of English, and I certainly never imagined I'd be writing a cookbook. Back then, my focus was on surviving in a new country and learning to make the kind of meals that would help me keep my family together, to make everyone feel loved and welcomed. But life has a funny way of surprising us, doesn't it? All those years spent cooking, learning, and experimenting; the long hours in the kitchen; and the lessons I passed on to my children—and later down the road, to my internet grandchildren—those moments are the foundation of this book. And although I never imagined I would be here, sharing these recipes with you all, it's a beautiful dream come true.

As I think about everything I've learned, I remember my mother back in Sarno, Italy. She never had a cookbook to follow, yet she knew how to make every dish with such love and care. I watched her work her magic, and as I did, I began to develop my own style. It was always about more than just cooking for me—it was about honoring my roots and ensuring that those lessons stayed alive. So I've spent decades perfecting the art of cooking, keeping our family's traditions strong, raising children, and, yes, learning new things along the way. But this book? This is my way of passing it all down to you.

This book is as much for you as it is for me. It's a way for me to share everything I've learned, so you can carry on our family's traditions and keep our meals alive in your own kitchens. The recipes you'll find here aren't just for special occasions; they're for every day. They're especially for Sundays, when you're gathered with loved ones, laughing around the table, or when you're making a meal for yourself because food is not just about nourishment; it's about love and about connection. Every dish in these pages tells a story, and I hope that when you cook with this book, you'll soak in the history and stories that have been passed down through the years.

The first part of this book is my story: how a young girl from Sarno found her way to America and how food became the bridge between past and present. It's a tale of love, hardship, and resilience, and it's not always an easy one to tell. But I hope that as you read it, you'll see not just the struggle, but also the beauty that comes from embracing change and finding new ways to hold on to what matters most. The strength I have today is built from the love and sacrifices of the past, and in this book, I share that with you. This is my legacy—our legacy.

Then, we move on to my Sunday dinner essentials. In this section, I share all the secrets I've picked up during the years, from the kitchen tools that make cooking easier to the little tricks that turn a simple meal into something special. Hosting Sunday dinners is about more than the food; it's about creating a space where family feels at home, where warmth and laughter abound. You'll find tips on everything from setting the table to ensuring the meal flows smoothly—because hosting a Sunday dinner is not just about cooking, it's also about making memories.

After that, we dive into the antipasti section, where you'll learn all the little bites and starters that make every meal feel like a feast. These appetizers are the perfect way to kick off any gathering, whether it's a big family meal or a quiet night with a few close friends. Then, we have the primi piatti, or first courses, which include all of my favorite pasta dishes, risottos, and a few other classics that bring the taste of Italy to your table. You'll also find some of the dishes that made me fall in love with cooking in the first place.

Next comes the secondi piatti, the heart of the meal. This section is where you'll find the hearty, soul-satisfying entrées that are a staple in both Italian and Italian American kitchens. These dishes are all about warmth, comfort, and of course, flavor. And then there's the insalate section, where you'll discover salads that are both traditional and modern. I've also included my favorite contorni, or side dishes, because no meal is complete without the perfect accompaniment.

And of course, we end with dolci—because what's a meal without something sweet to finish it off? These desserts are my way of sharing a little sweetness with you all, and I hope you'll savor every bite, just like I've done with my family all these years.

This book isn't just about recipes; it's also about love, family, and tradition. It's about honoring the past while looking to the future. I've poured my heart into every page, and I hope you feel that love when you cook from this book. When you prepare these dishes, I want you to know that you're carrying on the traditions that have kept our family close all these years. Cooking is an act of love, and this book is my way of passing that love on to you.

The table is set, and the wine is poured. Let's cook together.

Nonna Gracie's Story

I will never forget the day I arrived in New York City. Seasick after a solo eight-day voyage across the Atlantic, we docked on the west side of Manhattan. My first destination was Times Square. This is a moment that's forever etched into my memory—buildings bigger than I could imagine, thousands of people hurrying around, and advertisements plastered onto massive billboards. I didn't even know what an advertisement was then (and little did I know how familiar I'd become with them later!).

My Early Years

I was born in 1943 in Sarno, a small town in Campania, Italy, nestled near a mountain. Back then, Sarno was a place where everyone knew each other—the whole town was like family to me, and I to them. My parents owned a dairy store, selling mostly cheese and milk but also meat from their herd of goats at Easter. It wasn't a big money-making business. Instead, most deals were done by trading with other local shops. People weren't focused on getting rich; survival was what mattered most. Just before I was born, the bombings of World War II had destroyed many homes and businesses in my town, including my parents' and grandparents'. Adding to the hardship, a typhoid outbreak hit around the same time. Sadly, between birth complications and typhoid, my parents lost their first six children. The last passed away just two days before I was born.

ME AT 3 YEARS OLD!

Despite all of this, our family stayed strong and positive. Ironically, the shared tragedies made our family and our community stronger and safer because the only way to move forward was for everyone to work together and help each other. Ours was a self-sufficient town, where everyone poured their heart into doing their part. And as people grew older, their children took over for them and continued the family businesses.

The Importance of Tradition

Tradition was the heart of our community. We spent time with family on Sundays after church, made a year's supply of tomato sauce every August, and celebrated holidays with family. All of these and other traditions had one thing in common: food.

A SCENE FROM MY BACKYARD WEDDING.

MY AUNT MAKING HOMEMADE BREAD.

THIS IS ME, PICKING FRESH VEGETABLES TO FEED OUR FAMILY'S GOATS.

Sunday dinner was special because it happened every week. Even when life was tough, we always looked forward to Sunday. Even today, Sundays are a day to focus on what really matters. It's a time to connect with the people we love the most.

A Ten-Year-Old Chef

My parents were busy running their business, so at ten years old, I was given the responsibility of cooking our Sunday dinners. On Sunday mornings, my mother gave me a quick explanation of what to do, left the ingredients in the kitchen for me, and went to work with my father.

Sunday dinners weren't just about our normal family dinners but also about bringing together our extended family, friends, and other people from our town. After church, everyone would gather at our house, and it became my responsibility to cook for them all. This was how I learned to make Sunday sauce (a traditional pasta sauce that includes various meats), homemade pasta, meatballs, braciole, and many other classic Italian Sunday-dinner dishes.

As a ten-year-old chef, my dishes sometimes came out sciancato (or a little messed up), but the experience sparked my love for cooking. Speaking of sparks, I also had to learn how to cook over an open fire because we didn't have a stove. And I often used solid copper pots and pans that were cumbersome. It was challenging, but it was all we had and all I knew.

My mother, sister, and I weren't professional chefs—and we're still not. We learned to cook with simple ingredients from our land. Our strength isn't in fancy culinary skills. In fact, culinary schools and "professional" chefs often disagree with our style. Our strength is in simplicity, love, and decades-old recipes that most people enjoy more than complex dishes from Michelin-star restaurants.

PHOTOS OF ME THAT MY HUSBAND TOOK DURING HIS FIRST TRIP TO ITALY.

My Teenage Years

Throughout my teenage years, I perfected the recipes that my mother taught me by cooking every day. When my youngest sister, Antonietta, was old enough, she started helping me. As girls, we only went to school for a few years. After that, we became homemakers like my mom, aunts, cousins, and other women in our community. Meanwhile, my younger brothers, Antonio and Michele, worked with my dad.

No matter how long our days were, we always reunited at the dinner table. Every night we shared this precious time, talking about our days, our friends, and the good times and the bad.

Family Separation

In the early 1960s, many people from my town began moving to America with the hopes of greater opportunities. All I knew were stories about a country far away, but it seemed like a good idea, and my family thought so, too. We couldn't afford to move all at once, so we had to split up. Around this time, my father and my brother, Antonio, left Sarno for America to seek a better life for our family.

After arriving in New York City, my father got a job assembling tables and chairs at a factory on 149th Street in the Bronx. Antonio began working at night as a busboy at a restaurant in Westchester, just north of the Bronx. Moving to America also gave my brother the chance to go back to school during the day.

Our house in Sarno felt incomplete with part of our family so far away in America. Although we were separated, we looked forward to the day we would be together again. We didn't know when, but we knew that it would happen, and that there was light at the end of the tunnel. We kept up to date by writing letters to each other every month as we went about creating a new life.

Falling in Love

It wasn't like this for everyone, though. My cousin Domenico's family moved to America a generation before mine did. After fighting in World War II on the American side, Domenico decided to come visit us in Sarno. He brought with him his friend John, who was from Ohio. John's ancestors had immigrated from Sicily many years before. He was the first American-born person I had ever met.

MY HUSBAND, JOHN, AS A YOUNG MAN IN AKRON, OHIO.

I spent a lot of time with John that summer of 1961. He was handsome and caring and got along well with my family, even though there was a bit of a language barrier. He told stories about the war and showed us the medals he had received for his bravery. He also told us all about Ohio and his new home in Brooklyn.

John and I quickly fell in love. Before he went back home at the end of the summer, he asked me to marry him and join him in America. Of course, I said yes! It was a beautiful chance to start a family of my own, even though moving across the world scared me. John and I had a simple, joyful wedding in my aunt's backyard with our loved ones. After the wedding, my new husband returned to New York alone and waited for me to join him.

ME, JOHN, AND THE FAMILY ON OUR WEDDING DAY.

Coming to America

On September 25, 1961, when I was just 18 years old, I said goodbye to my mother, sister, and brother and boarded the SS *Leonardo da Vinci*, an ocean liner that sailed from Naples to New York City, all by myself. Some people flew to the States, but we didn't have that kind of money, so I had to take a ship. Even though Sarno was only 23 miles from the Mediterranean, this was my first time seeing the ocean. Only rich people had cars, so we usually only went places to which we could walk.

To be honest, I was terrified. I was traveling alone to a place halfway across the world that I had only heard about. But if I wanted to reunite with my new husband, my father, and my brother, this trip was something I had to do. Onboard I had a small cabin, which was about the size of a small closet, that included a cot. Although the ship was beautiful, the trip to New York was not "smooth sailing." Until October 2, my days were full of nausea and vomiting. But I made it to the land of hopes and dreams.

When I got off the boat in New York City, I was cheerfully greeted by my family, who quickly showed me Times Square. My first impression of New York was one of sheer terror. I didn't know buildings that big could even exist. *How do they stand like that? What if they fall?* The next thing I noticed were the busy streets. People by the thousands were hurrying around, in a big rush. Or maybe tens of thousands? I'd never seen that many people in my entire life, let alone in one place. The last thing I noticed in Times Square was the billboards. Not only had I never seen one, but I also didn't know what an advertisement was. With no big business in Sarno, there wasn't a place for marketing. But here I was, in the heart of New York City, staring at a billboard I couldn't read, wondering, *What have I done?*

LEFT: AN OLD PHOTO OF MARIO'S RESTAURANT ON ARTHUR AVENUE IN THE BRONX. JOHN WORKED THERE AS A WAITER WHEN WE LIVED IN THE AREA; CENTER: THE LEGENDARY MADONIA BAKERY ON ARTHUR AVENUE DURING THE GLORY DAYS OF THE BRONX'S LITTLE ITALY; RIGHT: A PHOTO OF ME IN UPSTATE NEW YORK ON MY FIRST LITTLE GETAWAY AFTER MOVING TO AMERICA.

My New Life

My adjustment to living in America wasn't easy. We didn't have GPS-equipped smartphones back then, of course, so doing things as simple as getting around was difficult. I didn't speak any English, so I could hardly communicate with anyone. Luckily, my husband was a native English speaker and spent a lot of time teaching me. His biggest suggestion was to watch TV and listen to the radio, which were new luxuries for me. The first English phrase I learned was from *I Love Lucy*, one of my favorite TV shows. One day, when John got home from work, I greeted him with a loud and proud "Hello, big boy!" My family still laughs about that.

John and my younger daughter, Rosalie, enjoying Sunday Dinner.

John was able to support us both with his salary as a waiter at a restaurant called Mario's of Arthur Avenue in the Bronx, which was my new neighborhood. So while learning a new language and a new city, my first job in the United States was the same as it had been back home: being a homemaker and doing the shopping, cooking, and cleaning. I quickly made friends with my neighbor, Mariarosaria, who was in the same position as me. She spoke little English, was new to the country, and was also a stay-at-home wife. We leaned on each other as we struggled to navigate our new lives. Oftentimes, we went to the supermarket together or cooked in each other's kitchens. Sharing this experience created a close bond between us. To this day, she's still one of my best friends.

Me and my daughters, Linda and Rosalie.

A year after I arrived in the United States, my mom and younger siblings were finally reunited with us. Although the setting was a bit different, we returned to what was most important: family time. Sunday dinner was back!

Fast-forward a few years, and John and I had two beautiful daughters, Linda and Rosalie. When both girls were in school, I decided it was time for me to get a job. I still had to be a homemaker, so my options were limited. My best choice was working in a school, so I became a substitute teacher at the public school where my younger daughter, Rosalie, started kindergarten. Eventually, I became the assistant to the principal. I loved the job, and I slowly improved my English and made more friends.

Life was good! I had a steady job, I spoke decent English, and my husband and I were raising our beautiful children. But that was when tragedy struck and my life was changed forever.

The Worst Days of My Life

In 1984, John was diagnosed with non-Hodgkin's lymphoma. Even worse, the doctors caught it too late. Within three months of the bad news, I buried the love of my life and was left to finish raising my two daughters alone. This was a tragic time for the three of us. Even though I was grieving, I had to be strong, especially for my daughters. Aside from offering emotional support, it was time for me to provide more financial support, too, which I wasn't prepared for.

I scrambled to find ways to make more money and quickly took on more jobs. Unfortunately I had to leave my part-time job at the school after fifteen years, but instead I found a full-time job as a housekeeper at St. Barnabas Hospital in my neighborhood. It paid more, but it still wasn't enough. So I got a second job as a nighttime housekeeper at Emigrant Savings Bank, where I would go to work after leaving the hospital.

I did this for decades. Although it was a struggle in every way, I'm really proud of what I accomplished and how strong it made me. Through these experiences, the shy, intimidated girl from a small town in southern Italy became a strong, independent woman. My personality changed over time because it had to. I was driven to succeed, to be a mom, and to play the role of the father my kids were missing. I wasn't going to let anything stop me.

JOHN AND ME ON OUR FIRST VACATION TO BERMUDA.

FAMILY TIME AFTER SUNDAY DINNER AT OUR HOUSE IN THE BRONX.

Becoming a Nonna

Eventually, Linda and Rosalie married my now sons-in-law, Eugene and John. Rosalie was the last to get married, and with the same family-first mentality our family always followed, she and John wouldn't let me live alone. So we got a two-family home together. In the meantime, Linda and Eugene made me a nonna. Seeing my first grandson, Anthony, for the first time was one of the most magical moments of my life. Becoming a grandparent felt like the reward for all those hard years, a token of success. After decades of work, I was able to retire and spend many of my days with Anthony and my four other grandchildren: John, Kristen, Matt, and Joe.

Being a nonna felt like I was getting a second chance at being a mom, but without most of the stressors I faced in my thirties and forties. I spent my days doing housework, cooking, and spending quality time with my family—all the things I loved! As the kids grew older, I introduced them to Sunday dinner, the annual tomato sauce jarring day in August, and many of the other traditions I grew up with.

Helping raise my grandchildren was an incredible experience for me. To this day, my grandchildren are some of my best friends. I remember a time when all of them slept in bed with me at once. I recall doing arts and crafts with them, cooking for them, and taking them to the park. I'll never forget when they brought friends over after school, and I would cook a full meal for them as an afternoon snack.

I like to think that I taught my grandchildren a lot. I helped teach them how to walk and talk. As they grew older, I taught them about the importance of family, our traditions, and Italian culture. I always emphasized the importance of God. What I later realized is that as much as they were learning from me, I was also learning from them.

Becoming the Internet's Italian Grandma

At the end of 2020, my grandson Matt, who already had a career making social media videos, asked me to share my cooking and story on camera. For months I hesitated. I was afraid. What if people made fun of my accent? What if they didn't like my cooking, which had always meant so much to me? What if they found me or my stories boring? But Matt persisted, and eventually I gave in.

At the time, I didn't realize how important this project would turn out to be. I had recently lost my little sister, Antonietta, and six months later, little brother, Antonio, unexpectedly passed away. Dealing with these losses turned my world upside down for a few years. For the first time, I questioned the meaning of everything. It occurred to me that sharing the gifts of family and tradition that I cherished as a child might give me a new sense of purpose.

Truthfully, although my heart was always full of love for my family, I never felt like I had achieved anything significant in the outside world. Working primarily with doctors and schoolteachers all of my life, I often felt inferior because I lacked their traditional education. Back then, long years of schooling and becoming "smarter" seemed to be the only way to make a positive impact in society. Making videos, however, has shown me that I can reach more people than I ever imagined possible.

My First Videos

I remember making biscotti in my first video. I was so nervous, but I didn't want to disappoint my grandson, so I pushed through it. Baking biscotti was so ordinary to me, but I didn't realize how special it could be to people who weren't familiar with it. Later, Matt told me that the video was seen by more than 300,000 people. I couldn't believe it—actually, the number was so big that it was hard for me to understand.

After that, Matt came to my kitchen every week to make a new video. In my second one, I made bread, another "normal" thing I had been baking for about 65 years. That video got nearly 1 million views. Within a month, I had 10,000 followers. I didn't really understand what this meant, but Matt assured me it was great, so we kept going. In just two or three months, I had 100,000 followers, thanks to videos like "Eggs in purgatory," which got more than 7 million views.

I was enjoying myself, I was gaining confidence, and I was beginning to create a real community of people who wanted to learn from me. The main thing, though, is that I felt compelled to return to TikTok every week for my "internet grandchildren."

Online Success

Understanding social media was really hard for me at first. Honestly, I still don't fully get it. I don't even have a smartphone (although I recently got an iPad for Christmas—I'm learning!) The numbers of followers, views, likes, and shares on my videos still don't make much sense to me. But I always enjoy hearing Matt read some of the hundreds of thousands of comments and messages we receive.

Eventually, these comments and messages started affecting my daily life. People at the grocery store wanted to take pictures with me, talk to me, hug me. Strangers at the clothing store said they loved me. Famous podcasts invited me on as a guest. Celebrities reached out on Instagram and complimented my videos. It was chaos for me—at 80 years young, achieving this level of recognition was something I had never imagined. All of this madness led to some amazing opportunities, like writing this book for you!

Within months of my first video, I landed my first brand partnership. Luckily, Matt had experience with this because I was clueless. I didn't understand how or why, but a company wanted to pay me thousands of dollars to talk about their product. It felt like free money. I made a great recommendation to my internet grandchildren, which they appreciated, and somehow I got paid. Matt continued to arrange partnerships for me, and suddenly I was a business owner—another thing I never thought possible for someone like me!

In May 2023, Matt and I were invited to a movie premiere. We walked the red carpet with what felt like hundreds of cameras flashing and reporters calling my name. We sat in a movie theater surrounded by A-list celebrities like Robert De Niro and people who inspire me, like Martha Stewart. We even went to the after-party and stayed out until one in the morning.

Times Square, Revisited

As unbelievable as the red carpet experience was, the most memorable moment that's occurred as a result of Matt and me making videos happened a year earlier, in May 2022. Matt told me we were going to dinner in New York City with a family friend. What I didn't know was that a company had paid for a billboard in Times Square featuring a picture of the two of us. As we walked to "dinner," I looked up and saw it—a picture of me and my grandson on one of the biggest billboards in Times Square. I was truly shocked. We celebrated with my whole family, taking pictures with the billboard in the background.

Standing there, surrounded by family and seeing myself on the big screen, I couldn't help but reflect on my first time in Times Square, just after my arrival from Italy decades ago. Back then, I stood in the same place, feeling a different kind of shock—culture shock, fear of the city's size, and some regret for leaving my comfortable homeland. Now, 60 years later, I was literally at the top of the place that once intimidated me the most. This full-circle moment made me feel not only successful but also finally a part of this city. I still get choked up when I think about it.

A Note to All of My "Grandchildren"

Undoubtedly, the most crucial part of this journey has been you. Your enthusiasm for my videos has kept us going. Without you, none of this would have been possible. This book also owes its existence to the millions of internet "grandchildren" who support me every day. I owe it all to you. Thank you from the bottom of my heart—you've changed my life in ways you may never realize.

Through my videos, I aim to shine a spotlight on Italian culture. Whether or not you're Italian, I hope you cherish the insights into our way of life, our traditions, and, of course, our cuisine. More than that, when you watch my videos, I want you to feel like one of my grandchildren, sharing in the love and care I put into every dish to nourish you.

As for this book, I hope it becomes a North Star for your Sunday dinners. Enjoy these cherished recipes, most of which have been part of my family for more than a century. Many of these dishes aren't found in fancy restaurants, but that's beside the point. These are the meals I would proudly serve you if you were sitting at my table for Sunday dinner.

Most importantly, I hope you savor these moments with the special people in your life. In a world where communities and families often grow apart, I hope this book inspires you to gather your loved ones around the dinner table, just as I have done my entire life.

Welcome to *Sunday Dinner with Nonna Gracie.*

Sunday Dinner Essentials

The Tools That Never Let Me Down

A good kitchen doesn't need to be fancy—it needs to be functional. You wouldn't believe how much amazing food came out of our minimalist kitchen when I was younger.

Although I believe your hands are always the *best* tools to use in the kitchen, they aren't the *only* ones. Here are the kitchen essentials I use every day:

- **Cast-iron skillet.** When it's seasoned properly, there's nothing better for searing meat or frying eggplant than cast iron. If you invest in quality, your cast-iron skillet will stick with you for a long, long time.
- **Colanders and fine-mesh sieves.** You'll use these tools more often than you think, whether for draining pasta or rinsing beans.
- **Digital thermometer.** Don't guess when it comes to the internal temperature of meat. A digital meat thermometer will save you every time.
- **Good cutting boards.** I like wooden cutting boards. To care for your wooden cutting boards, wash them quickly after use with mild soap and warm water, then dry them upright. I regularly rub them with food-safe mineral oil to prevent cracking and warping. (I have a separate board just for garlic and onions so it doesn't make my cookies taste funny.)
- **Grater.** I recommend having a larger grater for cheese and a smaller microplane or zester for grating ingredients like garlic, nutmeg, or lemon zest.
- **Heavy-bottomed pots and pans.** For sauces, soups, and braises, heavy pots help everything cook evenly. These are a must!
- **Kitchen shears.** I always have a pair of kitchen shears on hand for cutting herbs, snipping sausage, and cleaning chicken. They're much stronger and sharper than a normal pair of scissors.
- **Mixing bowls.** It's helpful to have a set of glass mixing bowls in different sizes. You'll always be reaching for one.
- **Sharp knives.** I always say that a dull knife is more dangerous than a sharp one.
- **Slotted spoon.** Whenever I make a sauce that needs pasta water, I always transfer the pasta with a slotted spoon instead of draining it in a colander. It keeps that precious, starchy water on the pasta.
- **Tongs.** They're like an extension of your hands. They're useful for tossing and serving salads and flipping meat and other ingredients in hot skillets.
- **Wooden rolling pin.** I use a rolling pin for rolling out sheets of fresh pasta dough or pizza dough. It's all about touch and control: The rolling pin tells me when the dough is ready!
- **Wooden spoons.** I have a drawer full of wooden spoons in various sizes. They don't scratch your pots, they feel good in your hand, and they get better with age.

Cooking Techniques and Secrets

(What My Mamma Taught Me, and I'm Passing On to You)

Little things can make a big difference in how your food turns out. My mother taught me that patience is an ingredient, and I truly believe that to be true. Here are some other lessons my mamma taught me that I'm passing on to you:

- **Don't rush the soffritto.** The slow cooking of onions, carrots, and celery is the base of so many great dishes, like my Tagliatelle Bolognese (page 107) and Osso Buco (Braised Veal Shanks) (page 128). Let it take its time; it will be ready when the veggies are soft and fragrant.
- **Taste as you go.** Especially for beginners, don't be embarrassed to taste as you go. A little taste here and there will help you know exactly what your dish needs.
- **Use your hands.** Whether you're mixing meatballs or kneading dough, your hands tell you more than any spoon can.
- **Let your meat rest.** After roasting, give your meat time before cutting into it to rest so it retains its juices.
- **Never overcrowd the pan.** Whether you're frying or sautéing, crowding the pan drops the temperature and ruins the sear. Work in batches as necessary for the best results. Abbi pazienza, figlio mio. (Be patient, my son.)
- **Layer your seasoning.** Don't wait until the end of a recipe to add salt. Season each component as you go for the best depth of flavor. You can always add more salt, but you can't take it out once it's in there.
- **Save your pasta water.** A splash of that starchy pasta cooking water can help thicken sauces and make them cling to your pasta like a dream. That said, it's easy to forget, so be sure you keep it top of mind when you're cooking pasta.
- **Cheese isn't just a topping.** Grated Pecorino Romano or Parmigiano-Reggiano can be stirred into a sauce for richness. Or add cheese to your breadcrumbs to give a little extra flare to dishes like breaded cutlets.
- **Let your dough rise properly.** Provide your yeasted doughs with a warm, draft-free place and some patience, and they will reward you with a finished bread that has real character.
- **Don't throw out the bones.** Whether beef, chicken, or pork bones, you can roast them, simmer them, and make a flavorful broth. That's liquid gold right there.

My mother always said, "Cook with your heart but trust your instincts." If something doesn't smell right, or if it feels off—listen to your gut.

Finding Good Ingredients That Make the Best Food

You can't make a great dish with poor ingredients. It's that simple. Here's what I look for when I'm shopping for Sunday dinner ingredients:

- **Olive Oil.** Use extra-virgin olive oil for finishing dishes and salads. Your oil should taste fresh and peppery, not flat or greasy. My recommendation, of course, is my own olive oil, Nonna's Olive Oil.
- **Produce.** Shop local when you can, and shop in season. For example, tomatoes in July can taste different from tomatoes in January. Smell them. Feel them. They should be heavy, fragrant, and ripe.
- **Meat and Poultry.** Get to know your butcher. Ask questions. Look for meat with good marbling (a bit of fat), especially when it comes to steaks and pork. Grass-fed and pasture-raised labels usually mean that the meat has better flavor and is better for you.
- **Seafood.** It should smell like the ocean, not fishy. If you can, buy it the same day you're cooking it. As with meat, get to know your fishmonger. Ask questions.
- **Cheese.** Buy blocks of cheese and grate them yourself. Preshredded cheeses often contain additives that keep them from clumping, and they don't melt the same.
- **Bread.** Buy it fresh from a local bakery or make your own. Good bread has a crust that crunches and a soft inside that's full of flavor.
- **Herbs.** Fresh is always best, but if you use dried, be sure they haven't been sitting in your cabinet for 10 years. Dried herbs lose a lot of flavor over time.
- **Canned Tomatoes.** Look for San Marzano or other Italian varieties. Fewer ingredients on the label is usually better.

It's also worth keeping a few pantry items always stocked: sea salt and kosher salt, whole black peppercorns (grind them fresh!), extra-virgin olive oil (can't go wrong with Nonna's Olive Oil), canned tomatoes, dried pasta, good vinegar, and fresh herbs if you can grow them. Fresh basil in a little pot by the window? A pot of fresh parsley in the backyard? That's gold.

The more you cook, the more you'll learn which ingredients are worth spending a little extra on. And when you taste the difference, you'll never go back.

Making Sunday Dinner Sacred for Your Family

Sunday dinner is sacred in my house. It's not just about food—it's about family, slowing down, and being together. Here are a few tips on making Sunday as important to your family as it is to mine:

- **Make it a ritual.** Choose a set time. Light some candles. Put on music. Make it feel different from the rest of the week.

- **Have a signature dish.** Maybe it's lasagna, or roasted chicken, or my Pork Braciole (page 92). Whatever dish you designate as Sunday dinner–worthy, when people smell it cooking, they know it's Sunday.

- **Invite others.** Whether it's family, neighbors, or friends who feel like family, invite them. Welcome them. The more, the merrier.

- **Cook together.** Give everyone a job, even if it's just tearing basil or setting the table. This can be helpful to you as you cook, but more importantly, it gives everyone a reason to spend more quality time together. (I'll get more into this in just a moment.)

- **No phones during dinner.** This is a big one. Everyone puts their phones away for the Sunday dinner meal. Focus on each other, on the food, and on your conversation.

- **Everyone comes hungry.** Don't let everyone fill up on snacks beforehand! A lot of work goes into Sunday dinner, and waiting to eat is part of paying respect to whomever prepared it.

- **Always send leftovers.** When your guests are back to work on Monday, they'll appreciate that little taste of yesterday's glory.

A tradition is just something you do more than once with intention. There's no blueprint for the perfect Sunday dinner, but if you make it your own and make it meaningful, you can consider it a success.

Tips for Hosting a Sunday Dinner

Hosting a Sunday dinner is about more than just the food—it's about creating an experience. Here are some tips I've learned during the years to make Sunday dinners as memorable and delicious as possible:

- **Have a clear menu.** It's tempting to make everything you love, but it's better to focus on a few key dishes that will really shine. When you're hosting, keep it simple with a few great recipes, and let the food speak for itself. I always like to have a couple of crowd-pleasers on the table—maybe a big bowl of pasta, a hearty meat dish or two, some sides that complement the main course, and of course, a few desserts to round things out.

- **Set the mood with music.** The right music can elevate the atmosphere of your dinner. It doesn't have to be fancy. I love to play something soft and cozy as guests arrive. Whether it's classic Italian tunes or just something relaxing, the music should be a background to the conversation, not the center of attention. (I like to play music that's on-brand for our dinner but that my guests don't listen to regularly. This helps them associate certain songs with the experience of Sunday dinner.)

- **Use the "serve yourself" method.** One of my favorite things about a Sunday dinner is making it a shared experience. Instead of stressing about plating each dish individually, set everything out on the table family style, and let everyone serve themselves. This keeps the atmosphere relaxed and invites more conversation. Plus, it makes people feel at home.

- **Don't overcomplicate the decor.** You don't need to overthink the table settings. A simple tablecloth, a few candles, and some fresh flowers can set a warm and welcoming tone at the table. It's the little touches, like a sprig of fresh rosemary or a bowl of olives on the table, that make everything feel special. Keep it simple, but make it feel intentional.

- **Make everyone feel like family.** Whether your guests are your closest relatives or friends who feel like family, be sure everyone feels welcome. Ask questions, tell stories, and don't forget to share a laugh or two. Sunday dinner is about more than just food; it's also about creating memories and strengthening those bonds that make us feel connected.

- **Leave room for leftovers.** Don't be afraid to make a little extra food! The best part about Sunday dinner is the leftovers. I always ensure there's enough to send home with my guests or to have the next day. There's nothing better than a second helping of Sunday dinner the day after.

- **Pour some wine.** Having a little bit of wine at Sunday dinner isn't about drinking. It's about celebration. It marks something sacred: family gathered, stories told, and food made with love. The wine isn't just for the glass; it's for the table. It's a symbol that says this moment matters.

Everyone's Welcome in My Kitchen

Involving family in the kitchen isn't just about getting help while you cook—it's also about teaching, bonding, and creating memories. So don't shoo everyone out of the kitchen while you work. Invite them in and give them something to do. Here are some ways to do that:

- **Start small.** Ask your kids or grandkids to wash the vegetables, tear the herbs, or measure the dry ingredients. In the beginning, especially for beginners, young family members, or those new to the family, this is a great way to involve your loved ones in the process. They'll feel helpful and proud to have been asked to assist.
- **Tell stories.** While you cook, share memories of who taught you the recipe, or the first time you made it. My grandchildren still recall the stories I told them when they were young.
- **Give them a signature dish.** Let each person be known for one thing they make really well—even if it's just salad!
- **Be patient.** Yes, it might get messy. And things might take longer. And you might have a bit more cleaning up to do than you usually would. But that's okay! Good things take a lot of work, and this is certainly no exception. In the end, it's all more than worth it.
- **Make it fun.** Put on music. Make a mess. Laugh. Share stories. Cooking doesn't have to be serious to be special.
- **Give them a taste.** Let them taste and decide if it needs more salt. It teaches confidence and trust.
- **Spill your secrets.** Share your little tricks, whether it's a splash of pasta water or the squeeze of lemon; they will appreciate and remember your lessons.
- **Give kids real jobs.** Even the little ones can sprinkle grated cheese, roll meatballs, or carry bread to the table. That's how traditions start.
- **Clean up together.** As the night unwinds, wash, dry, let the stories continue flowing, laugh, and continue having a good time. The cleanup is part of the tradition too.

Some of my best memories with my grandchildren are of them standing on a stool next to me, stirring sauce or sneaking bites of cheese. Following these simple tips will help you make similar memories for yourself and your family.

Setting the Table with Love

The table is where everything comes together. You don't need your Sunday dinner table to be fancy, but you do need to make it feel like something special. Here are a few ideas on how to set your table with love:

- **Use your good dishes.** Every Sunday is worth celebrating, so don't save your good dishes for the holidays. Get them out of storage. Tell your grandchildren the story of how you picked them out, or who you inherited them from.
- **Add a tablecloth.** If you don't normally use a tablecloth, now is the time. A pretty table covering can change the whole feel of the meal. And remember, you want to make Sunday dinners feel different from normal meals in your house.
- **Set the table early.** This helps get you in the mindset and makes it feel more intentional.
- **Include small touches.** Fresh bread in a basket, a little dish of olives, or a sprig of fresh rosemary can make all the difference.
- **Prepare the wine.** Even if it's an inexpensive bottle, opening a bottle or two of wine and pouring glasses signals the start of a slow, relaxing meal.
- **Include a bread basket.** Warm bread in a basket, wrapped up in a towel, is a Sunday dinner staple.
- **Put salt and pepper shakers on the table.** Salt and pepper on the table means everyone can season to their liking. Also, it looks thoughtful and old fashioned, like it always did when I grew up.
- **Leave room for the serving dishes.** Family-style eating brings everyone closer. Don't overcrowd the table—leave space to share.
- **Step back and take a look.** Before everyone arrives, look at what you've created—the warmth, beauty, and love. This also gives you a final chance to check your work and add anything you may have missed.
- **Light some candles.** Even if it's daylight, a little flame always makes a meal feel alive and special. It will also show your guests that you've focused on the details.

In the end, the best table is one that's full of love, laughter, and people who leave with full bellies and full hearts.

Happy cooking, and remember—cook with love, and you can't go wrong.

ANTIPASTI
(The Start)

Italian Charcuterie Board

An Italian charcuterie board, or tagliere di salumi e formaggi, is the perfect way to start a meal, setting the stage for what's to come. As a traditional Italian appetizer, it offers a little bit of everything—savory cured meats, rich cheeses, and tangy preserved vegetables—to awaken the palate without being too heavy. Whether served at a family gathering or for a special occasion, this board invites everyone to slow down, share, and savor the flavors of Italy before the main course arrives.

Prep Time:	Cook Time:	Total Time:	Serves:
15 minutes	None	15 minutes	4–6

Equipment

Large wooden board or platter
Small bowls
Cheese knife
Serving tongs
Small spoons (for spreads)

Ingredients

- 4 oz (115g) prosciutto di Parma, thinly sliced
- 4 oz (115g) soppressata, sliced
- 4 oz (115g) Parmigiano-Reggiano, cut into chunks
- 4 oz (115g) provolone Auricchio, sliced or cubed
- 4 oz (115g) ricotta salata, crumbled or sliced
- ½ cup pickled eggplant
- ½ cup pickled zucchini
- ½ cup roasted red peppers
- 1 cup Italian mixed olives
- ¼ cup sun-dried tomatoes (optional)
- ¼ cup toasted walnuts or Marcona almonds (optional)
- ¼ cup fig jam or honey (optional)
- 8–10 Italian breadsticks (or grissini)
- 1 small bunch fresh basil, for garnish

1. Arrange the prosciutto and soppressata in gentle folds or rolls on a large board or platter. Place the Parmigiano-Reggiano, provolone Auricchio, and ricotta salata in separate areas on the board, ensuring a balanced presentation.
2. Add the pickled eggplant, pickled zucchini, and roasted red peppers in small bowls or directly on the board in neat piles.
3. Place the olives in a small bowl and add to the board. Arrange the sun-dried tomatoes, toasted nuts, and fig jam or honey (if using) in separate bowls.
4. Lay the breadsticks along the edges of the board or in a small cup for easy grabbing.
5. Tuck the fresh basil leaves around the board for a pop of color and freshness.
6. Serve immediately with a selection of wines, such as a dry red Chianti or a crisp pinot grigio. Store leftover meats and cheeses wrapped tightly in the refrigerator for up to 3 days. Store the pickled vegetables and olives in airtight containers for up to 1 week.

Caprese Salad

Simple, fresh, and bursting with flavor, caprese salad is a true celebration of quality. The key is using the best ingredients you can find—ripe tomatoes; fresh, creamy mozzarella; and fragrant basil—and bringing them all together with a drizzle of rich, peppery extra-virgin olive oil. (If you really want to elevate this dish, use a high-quality olive oil like Nonna's Olive Oil. We make it with the same love and tradition that goes into all our family meals, ensuring each bite is as authentic as it gets.) Enjoy as a light appetizer or as a side dish, preferably with crusty bread to soak up the oil.

Prep Time:	Cook Time:	Total Time:	Serves:
10 minutes	None	10 minutes	2–4

Equipment

Knife
Cutting board
Serving platter

Ingredients

- 2 large ripe tomatoes, sliced into even rounds
- 8 oz (225g) fresh mozzarella, sliced into even rounds
- 10–12 fresh basil leaves
- 3 tbsp extra-virgin olive oil
- ½ tsp sea salt
- ¼ tsp freshly ground black pepper

1. Arrange alternating layers of tomato slices, mozzarella slices, and basil leaves on a serving platter.
2. Drizzle the olive oil evenly over the salad and then sprinkle with the salt and black pepper.
3. Serve right away; this salad is best enjoyed fresh. If needed, store leftovers in an airtight container in the refrigerator for up to 1 day.

Sausage & Broccoli Rabe Stromboli

This stromboli combines the savory flavors of sausage and broccoli rabe, wrapped in a golden, crispy dough. It's a simple and quick dish, especially if you use store-bought dough from your local pizzeria.

Prep Time:	Cook Time:	Total Time:	Serves:
20 minutes	40 minutes	1 hour	4–6

Equipment

Knife
Cutting board
Baking sheet
Parchment paper
Large pot
Colander
Large skillet
Slotted spoon
Rolling pin
Pastry brush

Ingredients

1 lb (450g) broccoli rabe, trimmed
2 tbsp extra-virgin olive oil
1 lb (450g) Italian sausage, casings removed
1 tsp salt
½ tsp freshly ground black pepper
½ tsp garlic powder
1 lb (450g) store-bought or homemade pizza dough
1 large egg, beaten

1 Preheat the oven to 365°F (185°C). Line a baking sheet with parchment paper.

2 Bring a large pot of salted water to a boil over high heat. Add the broccoli rabe, and blanch until bright green and tender, 2 or 3 minutes. Drain and set aside.

3 Heat the olive oil in a large skillet over medium heat. Add the sausage, breaking it up with a spoon, and cook until browned and cooked through, about 5 minutes. Season with the salt, pepper, and garlic powder.

4 Add the blanched broccoli rabe to the skillet with the sausage. Cook for 2 or 3 minutes, allowing the flavors to meld. Remove from the heat, and let the mixture cool slightly.

5 On a lightly floured surface, stretch and roll out the pizza dough into a large oval about ¼-inch (6mm) thick.

6 Starting with one edge of the dough, add about of the sausage and broccoli rabe mixture. Fold the dough over the filling and continue rolling, gradually adding more of the filling with each fold until all of the filling is used and the dough fully encloses the filling.

7 Transfer the stromboli to the prepared baking sheet. Brush the top with the beaten egg.

8 Bake for about 30 minutes, or until the crust is golden brown.

9 Remove from the oven and let rest for a few minutes before slicing. Serve hot. Store leftovers in an airtight container in the refrigerator for up to 2 days. Reheat in the oven at 350°F (180°C) for about 10 minutes or until warmed through.

Olive Bread

When I moved from Italy to New York, I discovered olive bread at Addeo & Sons Bakery on Arthur Avenue in the Bronx's Little Italy. Inspired, I decided to add olives to my family's generations-old bread recipe, and it's been a cherished treasure ever since. The unique ring shape of these olive bread pieces gives them an appealing appearance and ensures an even crust and soft interior, making them perfect for enjoying on their own or alongside your favorite Italian dishes.

Prep Time:	Cook Time:	Total Time:	Yield:
30 minutes (plus 2 hours rising time)	1 hour	1 hour, 30 minutes	3–4 pieces

Equipment

Large pastry board (optional)
Small bowl
Large mixing bowl
Kitchen towel or plastic wrap
Rolling pin
Baking sheet
Parchment paper
Pastry brush
Wire rack

Ingredients

3 cups all-purpose flour
1 cup 00 flour
1½ cups warm water (about 110°F/45°C)
0.25 oz (7g) packet active dry yeast, or 2¼ tsp active dry yeast
1½ tsp salt
2 (6-oz/170g) cans pitted whole black olives, drained
1 large egg, beaten

1. On a clean countertop or large pastry board, combine the all-purpose flour and 00 flour. Form a well in the center.
2. Mix the warm water with the yeast and salt in a small bowl until the yeast is dissolved. Pour the yeast mixture into the well in the flour. Using your hands, gradually incorporate the flour into the liquid until a shaggy dough forms.
3. Add the olives to the dough. Continue to knead the dough until the olives are evenly distributed and the dough becomes smooth and elastic, about 5 minutes.
4. Place the dough in a large, lightly oiled mixing bowl, cover with a kitchen towel or plastic wrap, and let rise in a warm, draft-free area until it doubles in size, 1½ to 2 hours.
5. When the dough has risen, punch it down to release any air bubbles. Divide the dough into 3 or 4 equal pieces, and roll each piece into a thick rope approximately 10 inches (25.5cm) long, then join the ends together to form a ring, pressing gently to seal. The rings should resemble rustic taralli or bagels.
6. Place the dough rings on a baking sheet lined with parchment paper, leaving space between each. Cover with a kitchen towel, and let rise again until slightly puffed, about 30 minutes.
7. Preheat the oven to 375°F (190°C).
8. Using a pastry brush, brush the tops of the dough rings with the beaten egg to give them a golden, glossy finish when baked.
9. Bake for about 1 hour, until the bread rings are a deep golden brown and sound hollow when tapped on the bottom.
10. Remove from the oven and transfer to a wire rack to let cool slightly. Serve warm or at room temperature. Store leftovers in an airtight container at room temperature for up to 2 days. For longer storage, freeze the olive bread in a freezer-safe bag for up to 1 month. Reheat in the oven at 350°F (180°C) for 10 to 12 minutes, or until warmed through.

Classic Rosemary & Sea Salt Focaccia

Focaccia has been a mainstay in my family for as long as I can remember. This bread is soft on the inside and golden brown on the outside, and a sprinkle of sea salt with fresh rosemary added just before it bakes makes the whole kitchen smell like home.

Prep time:	Cook time:	Total time:	Yield:
15 minutes (plus rising time)	25 minutes	40 minutes	1 large focaccia

Equipment

Large mixing bowl
Whisk
Plastic wrap
9 × 13-inch (23 × 33cm) baking sheet
Wire rack

Ingredients

- 2 cups warm water (about 100°F/40°C)
- 2 tsp dry yeast
- 2 tsp salt
- 5 tbsp extra-virgin olive oil, divided, plus more for greasing
- 4 cups 00 flour
- Flaky sea salt to taste
- 1 bunch of fresh rosemary, leaves stripped from stems

1. Whisk together the warm water, dry yeast, salt, and 2 tablespoons extra-virgin olive oil in a large mixing bowl until combined.
2. Add the 00 flour, and mix until the dough comes together and is smooth.
3. Cover the bowl with plastic wrap and set aside to rise. Every 30 minutes for 3 hours, stretch and fold the dough: Lift one side of the dough, stretch it upward, and fold it over itself. Repeat on all four sides. (Pro tip: To prevent sticking, wet your hands with water or olive oil first.)
4. After 3 hours of working the dough, cover the dough again and refrigerate overnight (or for at least 12 hours). Remove from the fridge 3 hours before baking to allow the dough to come to room temperature.
5. Heavily grease a 9 × 13-inch (23 × 33cm) baking sheet edge to edge with extra-virgin olive oil. Transfer the dough to the center of the greased baking sheet. Cover with plastic wrap, and let it rest for 30 minutes for one last rise.
6. Preheat the oven to 400°F (205°C).
7. Remove the plastic wrap and generously coat the top of the dough with the remaining 3 tablespoons olive oil. Gently stretch the dough to fit the baking sheet.
8. Using your fingertips, press all over the surface of the dough to create deep dimples. Sprinkle the top generously with the sea salt and rosemary leaves.
9. Bake for 25 to 30 minutes, or until the focaccia is golden brown and crisp on the top and on the edges.
10. Transfer to a wire rack and let cool slightly before slicing. Enjoy warm or at room temperature. Store leftovers in an airtight container in the refrigerator for up to 3 days. Reheat in the oven at 375°F (190°C) for about 10 minutes.

Tomato & Basil Bruschetta

Bruschetta has always been one of my favorite ways to start a meal. I love how something so easy—just a few fresh ingredients—can create such a bright and flavorful bite. I always toast my bread into crisp crackers, just like my mother did, so it holds up to the juicy tomato topping without getting soggy. This dish is always on the table at my family gatherings. Finish it with a drizzle of Nonna's Olive Oil to make all the difference!

Prep Time:	Cook Time:	Total Time:	Serves:
10 minutes	10 minutes	20 minutes	4–6

Equipment

Knife
Cutting board
Baking sheet
Pastry brush
Small bowl

Ingredients

1 French baguette, thinly sliced
3 tbsp extra-virgin olive oil
4 large ripe tomatoes, diced
10 fresh basil leaves, finely chopped
¼ cup finely chopped red onion
½ tsp sea salt
¼ tsp freshly ground black pepper
1 tbsp balsamic vinegar (optional)

1. Preheat the oven to 375°F (190°C).
2. Arrange the baguette slices in a single layer on a baking sheet. Brush each slice with olive oil.
3. Bake until golden and crisp, flipping halfway through, 8 to 10 minutes.
4. Add the diced tomatoes, basil, red onion, salt, pepper, and balsamic vinegar (if using) to a small bowl. Toss gently to mix.
5. Just before serving, spoon some of the tomato mixture onto each toasted bread slice and drizzle with a little more olive oil for extra flavor. Serve fresh for the best texture. Extra tomato mixture can be stored in an airtight container in the refrigerator for up to 1 day.

Mozzarella in Carrozza

When I was a child, my mother would make this dish as a special treat, especially when we had leftover bread that was just a little too dry to eat on its own. She'd dip the sandwiches in egg, fry them until golden and crisp, and serve them hot, with gooey mozzarella stretching between every bite. My parents owned a latticini (or dairy) store, so mozzarella usually wasn't hard to come by. For us, mozzarella in carrozza was comfort food—simple, delicious, and made with love. Now, whenever I prepare it, I'm reminded of those afternoons in our little kitchen in Sarno, watching my mother cook and waiting eagerly for that first warm bite.

PREP TIME:	COOK TIME:	TOTAL TIME:	SERVES:
10 MINUTES	10 MINUTES	20 MINUTES	2–4

Equipment

Knife
Cutting board
2 shallow bowls
Whisk
Large skillet
Tongs
Paper towels
Plate

Ingredients

8 slices white bread, crusts removed
8 oz (225g) fresh mozzarella, sliced
½ cup all-purpose flour
2 large eggs
1 tbsp salt
1 tsp freshly ground black pepper
¾ cup vegetable oil

1. Place four slices of the bread on a clean workstation. Evenly distribute the mozzarella over the bread, leaving a small border around the edges. Cover with the remaining four slices of bread to form sandwiches. Gently press down on each sandwich to help seal the edges.
2. Set up a dredging station using two shallow bowls. Add the flour in the first bowl, and whisk together the eggs, salt, and pepper in the second bowl.
3. Dredge each sandwich in flour, shaking off the excess. Then dip it into the egg mixture, ensuring it is fully coated.
4. Heat the vegetable oil in a large skillet over medium heat until it's shimmering.
5. Working in batches, use tongs to transfer the sandwiches to the oil. Fry the sandwiches until golden brown and crisp, 2 to 3 minutes per side. Transfer to a paper towel–lined plate to drain the excess oil.
6. Let cool slightly before serving. This is best enjoyed warm while the mozzarella is still gooey. Store leftovers in an airtight container in the fridge for up to 2 days. Reheat in a skillet over medium heat for 4 to 6 minutes for best results.

Fried Zucchini Fritters

There's something special about the way fried zucchini brings people together—it's crispy, savory, and impossible to stop eating. I slice mine extra thin, almost like shoestring fries, so they come out light and golden with a delicate crunch. Instead of breadcrumbs, I use just a bit of flour to create the perfect crunchy coating while letting the fresh zucchini shine. These fritters are best enjoyed hot, straight from the pan, with a squeeze of lemon and a sprinkle of sea salt.

Prep Time:	Cook Time:	Total Time:	Serves:
10 minutes	15 minutes	25 minutes	4–6

Equipment

Knife or mandoline
Cutting board
Large mixing bowl
Paper towels
Small mixing bowl
Large skillet
Slotted spoon
Plate

Ingredients

2 medium zucchini, cut into thin strips
½ tsp sea salt, plus more to season
½ cup all-purpose flour
2 large eggs, beaten
¼ tsp freshly ground black pepper
¾ cup vegetable oil
1 lemon, cut into wedges, for garnish

1. Add the zucchini strips to a large mixing bowl, and season lightly with salt. Let sit for a few minutes to release the excess moisture and then pat the zucchini and the mixing bowl dry with a paper towel.
2. Toss the zucchini with the flour in the same dry bowl, ensuring each piece is lightly coated.
3. Use a fork to beat the eggs in a small bowl, and season with the salt and pepper.
4. Heat the vegetable oil in a large skillet over medium-high heat until it reaches 350°F (180°C).
5. While the oil heats, dip the zucchini into the beaten eggs. Working in batches, carefully drop the zucchini into the hot oil. Fry until golden brown and crisp, 2 to 3 minutes.
6. Using a slotted spoon, transfer the fritters to a paper towel–lined plate to drain the excess oil. Sprinkle with a little extra sea salt while still warm.
7. Serve hot with lemon wedges on the side. These are best eaten hot and fresh, but if needed, store leftovers in an airtight container in the refrigerator for up to 1 day. Reheat in a dry skillet over medium heat for 4 to 6 minutes to crisp them back up.

MEATBALLS

Meatballs have always been a staple in my kitchen, and I make them just the way my family has done for generations. Mixing the meat by hand, frying the meatballs until golden brown, and letting them soak in a rich tomato sauce—there's no better way to enjoy these meatballs. Serve them with pasta, on a sandwich, or with a hunk of good bread to mop up the sauce.

PREP TIME:	COOK TIME:	TOTAL TIME:	SERVES:
20 MINUTES	1 HOUR, 30 MINUTES	1 HOUR, 50 MINUTES	6–8

EQUIPMENT

Knife
Cutting board
Small bowl
Large mixing bowl
Large skillet
Tongs
Paper towels
Plate
Large pot
Wooden spoon

INGREDIENTS

- 4 slices Italian round bread, crusts removed
- 1 lb (450g) ground pork
- 1 lb (450g) ground veal
- 5 large eggs
- 1 tsp salt
- 1 tsp freshly ground black pepper
- ½ cup grated Pecorino Romano, plus more for garnish
- ¼ cup chopped fresh parsley
- Vegetable oil, for frying

FOR THE SAUCE

- 4 tbsp extra-virgin olive oil
- 1 small yellow onion, diced
- 3 cups tomato purée (passata di pomodoro)
- ½ tsp salt
- ¼ tsp freshly ground black pepper
- ¼ cup chopped fresh basil

1. Place the bread slices in a small bowl, cover with water, and let soak for a few minutes. Squeeze out the excess water, and break the bread into small pieces.
2. Combine the ground pork, ground veal, eggs, soaked bread, salt, pepper, Pecorino Romano, and parsley by hand in a large mixing bowl until the mixture is uniform. Roll the mixture into meatballs about 3½ inches (9cm) round.
3. Add 2 inches (5cm) vegetable oil to a large skillet, and heat over medium heat. Working in batches, fry the meatballs, turning occasionally, until golden brown and cooked through, about 7 minutes. Use tongs to transfer the meatballs to a paper towel–lined plate to drain the excess oil. Set aside.
4. To make the sauce, heat the olive oil in a large pot over medium heat. Add the diced onion, and cook until softened and lightly browned, about 3 minutes.
5. Add the tomato purée, salt, pepper, and basil. Use a wooden spoon to stir well, and let the sauce simmer, stirring occasionally, for about 30 minutes.
6. Add the fried meatballs to the sauce and let them cook in the sauce, stirring occasionally to coat them evenly, for 30 to 45 minutes.
7. Remove the meatballs from the sauce and serve hot, topped with more sauce and grated Pecorino Romano. Store leftovers in an airtight container in the refrigerator for up to 3 days. Reheat gently in a medium frying pan over medium heat for 10 to 12 minutes before serving.

Eggplant Rollatini

When I was growing up in Sarno, ingredients weren't always available year-round like they are today in America. Eggplant was something we had only in the summertime, and because of that, every dish made with it was something special. This eggplant rollatini is one of my favorites—thinly sliced and fried eggplant is wrapped around a rich ricotta filling, covered in sauce, and baked to perfection. It's a dish that always brings back memories of those cherished summer meals.

Prep time:	Cook time:	Total time:	Serves:
30 minutes	1 hour, 15 minutes	1 hour, 45 minutes	4–6

Equipment

Large pot
Wooden spoon
Knife
Cutting board
Vegetable peeler
Large skillet
Paper towels
Plate
Large mixing bowl
13 × 9 × 2-inch (33 × 23 × 5cm) baking dish

Ingredients

4 tbsp extra-virgin olive oil
3 garlic cloves
3 cups tomato purée (passata di pomodoro)
¼ cup fresh basil leaves
1½ tsp salt, divided
½ tsp freshly ground black pepper, divided
2 large eggplants
Vegetable oil, for frying
1 cup all-purpose flour
2 cups ricotta
1 cup shredded low-moisture mozzarella
1 large egg
½ cup grated Pecorino Romano, plus more for topping
2 tbsp chopped fresh parsley

1. Heat the olive oil in a large pot over medium heat. Add the garlic and cook until golden brown, about 2 minutes.
2. Pour in the tomato purée and then add the basil, 1 teaspoon salt, and ¼ teaspoon pepper. Stir well and let the sauce simmer, stirring occasionally, for 30 minutes.
3. Meanwhile, prepare the eggplant. Trim off the top and then use a vegetable peeler to remove most of the skin, leaving some on for texture. Lay the eggplant on its side, and slice it lengthwise into thin strips.
4. Add 2 inches (5cm) vegetable oil to a large skillet and heat over medium heat.
5. Lightly coat each eggplant slice with the flour and then add to the skillet and fry in batches until golden brown, about 2 to 3 minutes per side. Transfer the eggplant to a paper towel–lined plate to drain the excess oil.
6. Combine the ricotta, mozzarella, egg, Pecorino Romano, parsley, the remaining ½ teaspoon salt, and the remaining ¼ teaspoon pepper in a large bowl until smooth.
7. Preheat the oven to 365°F (185°C).
8. Spread a layer of the tomato sauce on the bottom of the baking dish.
9. Lay a fried eggplant slice flat on a cutting board. Place 1 generous tablespoon ricotta mixture on the thicker end of the slice, and tightly roll the slice from top to bottom to enclose the filling. Repeat with the remaining eggplant slices and filling, arranging the rolled eggplant in a single layer in the baking dish.
10. Cover the rolled eggplant with more tomato sauce, and sprinkle with additional Pecorino Romano.
11. Bake for 30 minutes, or until heated through and bubbling.
12. Serve hot. Store leftovers in an airtight container in the refrigerator for up to 3 days. Reheat in the oven at 350°F (180°C) for 10 to 12 minutes, or until warmed through.

Zucchine Sott'olio

Equipment

Knife
Cutting board
Clean kitchen towels
Heavy pot or weight
Large bowl
Colander
Glass jar with lid

Ingredients

10 large zucchini
1 tbsp kosher salt
2 cups white vinegar
1 tsp dried oregano
1 small dried hot red pepper, crushed
2–3 garlic cloves, chopped
Extra-virgin olive oil, as needed

This is one of my favorite ways to preserve zucchini. Over time, the flavors of garlic, oregano, and red pepper infuse into the zucchini, making this dish a perfect addition to your antipasto spread. I vividly remember pairing the zucchini with pieces of toasted bread on many nights in my family's small Sarno home. Considering our limited resources at the time, these preserved zucchinis were easy to always have around. But don't be mistaken—the convenience of this dish doesn't diminish how enjoyable it is. These require a little patience to make, but once you taste them, you'll understand why it's worth the wait!

Prep time:	Cook time:	Total time:	Yield:
20 minutes (plus overnight drying time and 3 hours soaking time)	None	20 minutes	1 (24oz) jar

1. Peel the zucchini and cut them into quarters. Remove all the seeds. Cut the quarters into strips that are about ½ inch (1.25cm) thick.
2. Lay the zucchini strips on a clean kitchen towel, and sprinkle them with the kosher salt. Cover with another towel, and place a heavy pot or weight on top. Let the zucchini sit overnight to remove the excess moisture.
3. The next day, combine the vinegar with 1 cup water in a large bowl. Add the zucchini, and let soak for 3 hours.
4. Drain the zucchini and squeeze out any excess liquid with your hands. Lay them out to dry on a clean towel. Dry the bowl.
5. Toss the zucchini with the oregano, crushed red pepper, and garlic in the large dried bowl. Drizzle with a little olive oil, and mix well.
6. Pack the zucchini mixture tightly in a clean glass jar, pressing down as you go.
7. Pour the olive oil over the top until the zucchini are completely submerged. Seal the jar tightly, and store it in the refrigerator. Let the flavors develop for at least a few days before enjoying.
8. Keep refrigerated and use within a month. To maintain freshness, always ensure the zucchini remain fully submerged in the olive oil. If needed, add additional oil to the jar.

NONNAS

Eggplant Caponata Crostini

Eggplant caponata is a traditional Italian dish made with diced eggplant, celery, onion, tomatoes, and olives or capers, all slowly cooked in olive oil and finished with a sweet-and-sour balance of vinegar and sugar. This dish always reminds me of holidays and family parties. We make a big batch of caponata and serve it on toasted bread for everyone to snack on. It's sweet, tangy, and totally addictive.

Prep time:	Cook time:	Total time:	Serves:
15 minutes	45 minutes	1 hour	6

Equipment

Knife
Cutting board
Large skillet
Wooden spoon
Baking sheet

Ingredients

- ½ cup extra-virgin olive oil, divided, plus more for drizzling
- 2 medium eggplants, cut into ½-inch (1.25cm) cubes (about 1½ lb/680g total)
- ½ medium yellow onion, finely chopped
- 2 celery stalks, finely chopped
- 1 ??? red bell pepper, ribs and seeds removed, and chopped
- ¼ cup capers, drained
- ¼ cup green olives, chopped
- ¼ cup red wine vinegar
- 1 tbsp sugar
- 1½ cups crushed plum tomatoes
- Kosher salt to taste
- Freshly ground black pepper to taste
- 1 baguette, sliced into ½-inch (1.25cm) rounds
- Fresh basil, for garnish (optional)

1. Set a large skillet over medium heat, and add ¼ cup olive oil. When the oil is hot, add the eggplant and sauté until golden brown and tender, 10 to 12 minutes. Transfer to a large bowl and set aside.
2. In the same skillet, heat the remaining ¼ cup olive oil. Add the onion, celery, and red bell pepper, and cook until softened, 5 to 6 minutes.
3. Use a wooden spoon to stir in the capers, olives, vinegar, and sugar, and cook for 2 to 3 minutes, allowing the flavors to meld.
4. Add the crushed tomatoes and cook, stirring occasionally, for 10 minutes.
5. Return the cooked eggplant to the skillet. Season with salt and pepper, stir well, and simmer for 5 minutes. Remove from the heat and set aside to cool.
6. While the caponata cools, preheat the oven to 375°F (190°C).
7. Arrange the baguette slices on a baking sheet. Drizzle with the extra-virgin olive oil, and season with salt. Toast for 8 to 10 minutes, until golden and crisp.
8. To serve, spoon the caponata onto the toasted bread and garnish with fresh basil (if using). Serve at room temperature. Store leftovers in an airtight container in the refrigerator for up to 4 days. Toast the fresh crostini when ready to serve.

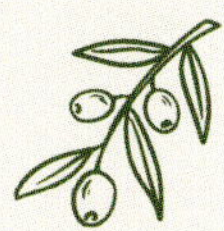

Stuffed Peppers

When I moved to New York, I made a dear friend who was from Naples, and she taught me how to make these stuffed peppers just like her family did back in Italy. Over the years, I've made a few refinements, but this recipe has now been in our family for more than 50 years. These peppers are filled with a rich, savory mixture of veal, rice, cheese, and herbs and then baked in a flavorful tomato sauce until perfectly tender. They're a comforting and hearty meal that everyone loves at Sunday dinner.

Prep Time:	Cook Time:	Total Time:	Serves:
20 minutes	1 hour, 30 minutes	1 hour, 50 minutes	4–6

Equipment

Knife
Cutting board
2 large skillets
Medium pot
Colander
Wooden spoon
Large mixing bowl
13 × 9 × 2-inch (33 × 23 × 5cm) baking dish

Ingredients

4 tbsp extra-virgin olive oil, divided
4 garlic cloves, minced, divided
4 cups tomato sauce
1 tsp salt, plus more to taste
½ tsp freshly ground black pepper, divided
¼ cup chopped fresh basil
1 cup white rice
1 lb (450g) ground veal
½ cup grated Pecorino Romano
2 tbsp chopped fresh parsley
2 large eggs
1 cup shredded low-moisture mozzarella
4 large red or yellow bell peppers

1. Preheat the oven to 375°F (190°C).
2. Heat 2 tablespoons olive oil in a large skillet over medium heat. Add half of the minced garlic, and cook until golden brown, about 1 minute.
3. Pour in the tomato sauce, season with the salt, ¼ teaspoon pepper, and the basil. Stir well and let simmer while you prepare the other ingredients.
4. Bring a medium pot of salted water to a boil over high heat. Add the rice and cook until tender, according to package instructions. Drain and set aside.
5. Heat the remaining 2 tablespoons olive oil in another large skillet over medium heat. Add the remaining minced garlic, and cook until golden brown, about 1 minute.
6. Add the ground veal, breaking it up with a wooden spoon, and sauté until browned and fully cooked, about 5 to 7 minutes. Remove the pan from the heat.
7. Combine the veal, rice, Pecorino Romano, parsley, eggs, mozzarella, and the remaining ¼ teaspoon pepper in a large mixing bowl until fully combined.
8. Cut the tops off the bell peppers, and remove the stems, seeds, and ribs. Generously stuff each pepper with the veal-and-rice mixture.
9. Coat the bottom of the baking dish with a layer of the simmering tomato sauce. Set the stuffed peppers upright in the dish and then carefully cover each with more tomato sauce.
10. Bake for 1 hour, or until they are tender and the filling is cooked through.
11. Remove from the oven and let cool slightly before serving. Enjoy hot with extra sauce on the side. Store leftovers in an airtight container in the refrigerator for up to 3 days. Reheat in the oven at 350°F (180°C) for about 10 to 12 minutes or until warmed through.

PRIMI PIATTI

(The First Course)

LASAGNA

This may not be your traditional lasagna, but I've been making it this way for more than 50 years. Layers of pasta, ricotta, sausage, and rich tomato sauce come together in a dish that's pure comfort. When it comes out of the oven bubbling and golden, you know you're in for something special.

PREP TIME:	COOK TIME:	TOTAL TIME:	SERVES:
30 MINUTES	2 HOURS	2 HOURS, 30 MINUTES	6–8

EQUIPMENT

2 large pots
Wooden spoon
Medium pot
Colander
Kitchen towel
Knife
Cutting board
Large mixing bowl
Tongs
13 × 9 × 2-inch (23 × 33 × 5cm) baking dish

INGREDIENTS

4 tbsp extra-virgin olive oil
1 small yellow onion, diced
3 cups crushed plum tomatoes
1½ tsp salt, divided
½ tsp freshly ground black pepper, divided
¼ cup fresh basil
8 Italian sausages
1 lb (450g) dry lasagna sheets
16 oz (450g) ricotta
2 large eggs
1½ cups grated Parmigiano-Reggiano, plus more for topping
2 cups shredded low-moisture mozzarella

1 Heat the olive oil in a large pot over medium heat. Add the diced onion, and cook until softened and golden brown, about 2 minutes.

2 Pour in the crushed plum tomatoes, and season with 1 teaspoon salt, ¼ teaspoon pepper, and the basil. Stir well and let the sauce simmer.

3 Meanwhile, bring a medium pot of water to a boil over high heat. Using a fork, poke small holes in the sausages and then add them to the pot. Boil for a few minutes to remove the excess fat and then transfer the sausages to the tomato sauce and cook for about 45 minutes.

4 When the sausages have cooked for about 30 minutes, preheat the oven to 375°F (190°C).

5 Fill another large pot with salted water, bring to a boil over high heat. Add the lasagna sheets, and cook until al dente, according to the package instructions. Drain the pasta, lay the sheets on a clean kitchen towel, and set aside to dry.

6 Add the ricotta, eggs, and the remaining ½ teaspoon salt and remaining ¼ teaspoon pepper to a large mixing bowl. Mix until smooth.

7 Using tongs, remove the sausages from the tomato sauce and slice them into rounds ⅓-inch (8.5mm) thick.

8 To assemble the lasagna, spread a layer of tomato sauce in the bottom of the baking dish. Add a layer of lasagna sheets, followed by a sprinkle of grated Parmigiano-Reggiano, several dollops of the ricotta mixture, the sausage slices, the shredded mozzarella, and more sauce. Repeat the layers until almost all the ingredients are used. Finish with a top layer of the remaining lasagna sheets, covered with the final bits of sauce and grated Parmigiano-Reggiano.

9 Bake for 1 hour, or until the lasagna is bubbling and golden brown.

10 Let rest for a few minutes before slicing into squares and serving hot. Store leftovers in an airtight container in the refrigerator for up to 3 days. Reheat in the oven at 350°F (180°C) for 15 to 20 minutes or until warmed through.

Penne Arrabbiata

This is a simple but bold dish, full of heat from the crushed red pepper and the rich flavor of homemade tomato sauce. The word *arrabbiata* means "angry" in Italian, referring to the fiery spice in this classic recipe. It's quick to make but always delivers big flavor.

Prep time:	Cook time:	Total time:	Serves:
10 minutes	25 minutes	35 minutes	4–6

Equipment

Large skillet
Wooden spoon
Large pot
Colander

Ingredients

4 tbsp extra-virgin olive oil
3 garlic cloves
1 small dried hot red pepper, crushed, or to taste
3 cups crushed plum tomato sauce
1½ tsp salt
½ tsp freshly ground black pepper
¼ cup fresh basil
1 lb (450g) penne pasta
Grated Parmigiano-Reggiano, for garnish (optional)

1. Heat the olive oil in a large skillet over medium heat. Add the garlic, and cook until golden brown, about 2 minutes.
2. Add the crushed dried red pepper to taste, pour in the tomato sauce, and stir. Season with the salt, the pepper, and the basil. Simmer the sauce for about 15 minutes.
3. Meanwhile, bring a large pot of salted water to a boil over high heat. Cook the penne until al dente, according to package instructions. Drain the pasta, reserving ½ cup pasta water.
4. Add the pasta to the sauce, and toss well to coat. If needed, stir in a splash of the reserved pasta water to loosen the sauce.
5. Serve hot with a generous sprinkle of Parmigiano-Reggiano (if using). Store leftovers in an airtight container in the refrigerator for up to 2 days. Reheat in a medium frying pan over medium heat for 5 to 7 minutes, adding a splash of water to loosen the sauce.

ORECCHIETTE
with Broccoli Rabe & Sausage

This dish is a classic in my kitchen. The orecchiette holds onto all the flavors of the garlicky olive oil, sausage, and broccoli rabe, making every bite perfect. There are few things more magical than the combination of broccoli rabe and sausage.

PREP TIME:	COOK TIME:	TOTAL TIME:	SERVES:
15 MINUTES	40 MINUTES	55 MINUTES	4–6

EQUIPMENT

Knife
Cutting board
Large skillet
Wooden spoon
Large pot
Colander

INGREDIENTS

4 tbsp extra-virgin olive oil
4 garlic cloves
1 lb (450g) Italian sausage, casings removed
1 tsp salt, divided
½ tsp freshly ground black pepper, divided
1 bunch of broccoli rabe, trimmed
1 lb (450g) orecchiette pasta

1 Heat the olive oil in a large skillet over medium heat. Add the garlic cloves, and cook until golden brown, about 2 minutes.

2 Add the sausage meat, breaking it up with a wooden spoon. Season with ½ teaspoon salt and ¼ teaspoon pepper. Cook until browned and fully cooked through, about 4 to 6 minutes. Transfer the sausage to a plate. Set aside.

3 Bring a large pot of salted water to a boil over high heat. Add the broccoli rabe, and blanch until bright green and tender, 2 or 3 minutes. Drain.

4 Add the blanched broccoli rabe to the skillet used for the sausage. Set over high heat, and sauté the broccoli rabe for a few minutes, allowing it to absorb the sausage flavor. Season with the remaining ½ teaspoon salt and remaining ¼ teaspoon pepper.

5 Bring another large pot of salted water to a boil over high heat. Cook the orecchiette until al dente, according to package instructions. Drain and set aside.

6 Return the sausage to the skillet with the broccoli rabe. Cook, stirring, over low heat to combine and let the flavors meld together.

7 Add the pasta, and toss everything together to evenly coat.

8 Serve hot. Store leftovers in an airtight container in the refrigerator for up to 2 days. Reheat in a skillet with a drizzle of olive oil over medium heat for 5 to 7 minutes.

CAMPANELLE *with Cauliflower*

This recipe is a delicious combination of tender cauliflower, rich tomato sauce, and perfectly cooked pasta. It's one of those meals that's been a staple in my family for many years. The cauliflower soaks up all the flavors of the sauce, making this a simple yet incredibly satisfying dish. I hope it's as special to your family as it's been to mine for the last few decades.

PREP TIME:	COOK TIME:	TOTAL TIME:	SERVES:
15 MINUTES	40 MINUTES	55 MINUTES	4–6

EQUIPMENT

Knife
Cutting board
Medium bowl
Large skillet
Wooden spoon
Large pot
Colander

INGREDIENTS

1 head cauliflower, cut into florets
¼ cup plus 1 tbsp extra-virgin olive oil, divided
1 medium yellow Spanish onion, sliced
14.5 oz (410g) can plum tomatoes, crushed, with juice
¾ tbsp salt, or to taste
Pinch of crushed red pepper flakes
Fresh basil (optional)
1 lb (450g) campanelle pasta

1 Add the cauliflower to a medium bowl, and cover with water. Set aside.

2 Heat ¼ cup olive oil in a large skillet over medium heat. Add the sliced onion, and sauté until golden brown, about 2 minutes.

3 Pour in the crushed plum tomatoes and 1 cup water. Bring to a boil and then reduce the heat to medium-low. Stir to combine.

4 Add the salt, crushed red pepper flakes, and fresh basil (if using).

5 While the sauce simmers, strain the cauliflower from its soaking water and add it to the skillet along with 1½ cups fresh water. Cover and let cook for 7 minutes.

6 Fill a large pot with salted water, set over high heat, and bring to a boil. Add the remaining 1 tablespoon olive oil.

7 After 10 minutes of the salted water boiling, add ½ cup of the salted water to the sauce and continue simmering.

8 Cook the campanelle in the boiling salted water until al dente, according to package instructions.

9 When the sauce has cooked for another 15 minutes, add the strained pasta to the sauce and stir well to combine.

10 Serve hot. Store leftovers in an airtight container in the refrigerator for up to 2 days. Reheat gently in a medium frying pan over medium heat for 5 to 7 minutes, adding a splash of water.

Lentil Soup

This soup is my favorite thing to eat on a cold winter day. Simple, nourishing, and packed with flavor, it's the kind of meal that brings everyone running to the dinner table. The lentils cook slowly with fresh vegetables and extra-virgin olive oil, creating a rich, comforting soup that can't be beaten on a cool day.

Prep Time:	Cook Time:	Total Time:	Serves:
15 minutes	45 minutes	1 hour	6–8

Equipment

Knife
Cutting board
Large pot
Wooden spoon

Ingredients

3 celery stalks, chopped
5 small plum tomatoes, chopped
2 garlic cloves, crushed
¾ cup extra-virgin olive oil
2 carrots, peeled and cut into small cubes
½ medium yellow onion, diced
1 lb (450g) lentils, rinsed
1½ tsp salt
½ tsp freshly ground black pepper
½ tsp dried oregano
¼ tsp crushed red pepper flakes (optional)

1. Bring 8 cups water to a boil in a large pot over high heat. Add the celery, tomatoes, and garlic, and pour in the olive oil. Bring to a boil again.
2. Add the carrots and onion, and cook for 5 minutes.
3. Add the lentils, and stir to combine. Reduce the heat to medium-low, and simmer, stirring occasionally, for 35 to 40 minutes.
4. Season with salt, pepper, oregano, and crushed red pepper flakes (if using). Stir and simmer for another 5 minutes.
5. Serve hot with a drizzle of extra-virgin olive oil and a slice of crunchy bread. Store leftovers in an airtight container in the refrigerator for up to 3 days. Reheat in a medium frying pan over medium heat for 7 to 9 minutes, adding a splash of water if needed.

PASTA *with Peas*

This simple yet flavorful dish is a comforting staple in my kitchen. When I was growing up, this was considered "peasant food" because it was inexpensive to make. In post–World War II Italy, money was tight, and meals like this—made with pantry staples—helped feed the family without breaking the budget. Don't let that fool you into thinking this is any less delicious than an expensive dish of pasta, though. The combination of sweet peas, savory double-smoked bacon, and rich tomato sauce makes for a delicious and satisfying meal. Cooking the peas low and slow in the sauce brings out their natural sweetness, while the tubettini pasta soaks up all the rich flavors. It's an easy meal that comes together beautifully every time.

PREP TIME:	COOK TIME:	TOTAL TIME:	SERVES:
10 MINUTES	40 MINUTES	50 MINUTES	4

EQUIPMENT

Knife
Cutting board
Large skillet
Wooden spoon
Large pot
Colander

INGREDIENTS

- 2 tbsp extra-virgin olive oil
- 4 oz (115g) double-smoked bacon, diced
- 1 small yellow onion, diced
- 2 cups tomato sauce
- ½ tsp salt, plus more to taste
- ¼ tsp freshly ground black pepper, plus more to taste
- ¼ tsp crushed red pepper flakes (optional)
- 2 cups fresh or frozen peas
- 1 lb (450g) tubettini pasta
- Freshly grated Pecorino Romano, for serving

1. Heat the olive oil in a large skillet over medium heat. Add the diced bacon and onion, and cook until the bacon is crisp and the onion is soft, 5 to 7 minutes.
2. Pour in the tomato sauce, and stir to combine with the bacon and onion. Season with the salt, pepper, and red pepper flakes (if using), and stir to incorporate. Cook for 2 minutes.
3. Stir in the peas, and cook, stirring occasionally, for 30 minutes.
4. Meanwhile, bring a large pot of salted water to a boil over high heat. Add the tubettini and cook until al dente, according to the package instructions. Drain the pasta, reserving about ½ cup pasta water.
5. Add the pasta to the skillet, and stir well to coat, adding a splash of reserved pasta water to loosen the sauce if needed. Season with salt and freshly ground pepper to taste.
6. Spoon into bowls and top with freshly grated Pecorino Romano. Serve immediately. Store leftovers in an airtight container in the refrigerator for up to 2 days. Reheat gently in a medium frying pan over medium heat for 5 to 7 minutes, adding a little water if needed to loosen the sauce.

Pasta e Fagioli

(Pasta & Beans)

This dish is simple, comforting, and made with humble ingredients that come together to create something special. When I make this, it reminds me of home—slowly simmering the beans, adding just the right seasonings, and finishing it off with tender pasta. Just one bowl may not be enough, especially on a chilly day.

Prep time:	Cook time:	Total time:	Serves:
10 minutes	1 hour, 30 minutes	1 hour, 40 minutes	4–6

Equipment

Knife
Cutting board
2 large pots
Wooden spoon
Colander

Ingredients

- 2 cups cannellini beans
- 1 cup tomato sauce
- 2 garlic cloves
- 1 stalk celery, chopped
- 3 tbsp extra-virgin olive oil, plus more for serving (optional)
- 1½ tsp salt
- ½ tsp freshly ground black pepper
- ½ tsp dried oregano
- 1 lb (450g) tubettini pasta

1. Add 6 cups water to a large pot and bring to a boil over high heat. Add the cannellini beans, and cook them for 5 minutes.
2. Stir in the tomato sauce, garlic, celery, olive oil, salt, pepper, and oregano. Reduce the heat to low, and let the mixture simmer, stirring occasionally, for about 1 hour, 30 minutes.
3. Meanwhile, bring a separate pot of salted water to a boil over high heat. Add the tubettini, and cook until al dente, according to package instructions. Drain the pasta.
4. Add the pasta to the soup, and stir well to combine, allowing the flavors to meld together.
5. Serve hot with an extra drizzle of olive oil (if using). Store leftovers in an airtight container in the refrigerator for up to 3 days. Reheat gently in a medium saucepan over medium heat for 5 to 7 minutes, adding a splash of water if needed.

Short Ribs Ragu

This slow-cooked short ribs ragu is rich, hearty, and full of deep flavor. The meat becomes fall-apart tender as it simmers in a sauce of tomatoes, red wine, and aromatics. Tossed with fettuccine, it's a dish that is sure to please.

PREP TIME:	COOK TIME:	TOTAL TIME:	SERVES:
20 MINUTES	4 HOURS	4 HOURS, 20 MINUTES	6–8

Equipment

Knife
Cutting board
Paper towels
2 large pots, or 1 large pot and 1 Dutch oven
Tongs
Wooden spoon
Colander

Ingredients

3 lb (1.35kg) bone-in short ribs
1½ tsp salt, divided
½ tsp freshly ground black pepper, divided
3 tbsp extra-virgin olive oil
1 large yellow onion, chopped
3 garlic cloves, minced
2 carrots, peeled and chopped
2 tbsp tomato paste
1 cup dry red wine
28 oz (800g) can crushed plum tomatoes
2 cups beef stock
1 lb (450g) fettuccine pasta
Grated Pecorino Romano, for garnish

1. Pat the short ribs dry with paper towels, and season them with 1 teaspoon salt and ¼ teaspoon pepper.
2. Heat the olive oil in a large pot or Dutch oven over medium-high heat. Add the short ribs, and brown them on all sides, about 2 to 3 minutes per side. Transfer the short ribs to a plate, and set aside.
3. Add the onion, garlic, and carrots to the pot, and sauté until softened, about 5 to 6 minutes. Season with the remaining ½ teaspoon salt and remaining ¼ teaspoon pepper.
4. Stir in the tomato paste and cook for 1 minute.
5. Pour in the red wine, scraping up any browned bits from the bottom of the pot. Cook for about 2 minutes to allow the alcohol to evaporate.
6. Add the crushed tomatoes and beef stock, and stir well to combine. Return the short ribs to the pot, submerging them in the sauce. Reduce the heat to low, cover, and simmer, stirring occasionally, for 3½ to 4 hours.
7. When the ragu is almost ready, bring a large pot of salted water to a boil over high heat. Cook the fettuccine until al dente, according to package instructions. Drain the pasta and set aside.
8. Remove the short ribs from the sauce and shred the meat, discarding the bones. Return the shredded meat to the sauce, and stir to combine.
9. Add the pasta to the ragu and toss to coat.
10. Serve hot with a generous sprinkle of grated Pecorino Romano. Store leftovers in an airtight container in the refrigerator for up to 3 days. Reheat gently in a medium frying pan over medium-low heat for 15 to 17 minutes, adding a splash of water or stock if needed.

Manicotti

Manicotti is a dish that always feels special. I love making it the old-fashioned way—with fresh pasta sheets, a rich ricotta filling, and a slow-cooked tomato sauce. Every bite is creamy, cheesy, and comforting, just the way it should be.

Prep time:	Cook time:	Total time:	Serves:
30 minutes	1 hour, 25 minutes	1 hour, 55 minutes	6–8

Equipment

Knife
Cutting board
2 large pots
Wooden spoon
Large mixing bowl
Paper towels
Colander
13 × 9 × 2-inch (33 × 23 × 5cm) baking dish

Ingredients

4 tbsp extra-virgin olive oil
1 small yellow onion, diced
3 cups tomato purée (passata di pomodoro)
2¼ tsp salt, divided
½ tsp freshly ground black pepper, divided
¼ cup fresh basil, leaves whole
32 oz (910g) container ricotta
1 cup shredded low-moisture mozzarella
¾ cup grated Pecorino Romano, plus more for garnish
2 large eggs
1 lb (450g) fresh manicotti sheets

1. Heat the olive oil in a large pot over medium heat. Add the diced onion, and cook until softened and lightly browned, about 2 minutes.
2. Pour in the tomato purée, and season with 1 teaspoon salt and ¼ teaspoon pepper. Stir in the basil, and let the sauce simmer, stirring occasionally, for 30 minutes.
3. Meanwhile, preheat the oven to 365°F (185°C).
4. Add the ricotta, mozzarella, Pecorino Romano, eggs, and the remaining 1¼ teaspoons salt and remaining ¼ teaspoon pepper to a large mixing bowl. Stir until well combined.
5. Fill another large pot with salted water, and bring to a boil over high heat. Add the fresh manicotti sheets, and cook until just tender, about 2 to 3 minutes. Drain and pat dry with paper towels.
6. Coat the bottom of the baking dish with a layer of the tomato sauce.
7. Place a generous amount of the ricotta mixture on one end of each pasta sheet, and roll tightly lengthwise. Set the rolled-up manicotti in the baking dish. Repeat with the remaining sheets and filling. Cover the rolled manicotti with more tomato sauce.
8. Bake for 45 minutes.
9. Remove from the oven and sprinkle with additional grated Pecorino Romano.
10. Serve hot. Store leftovers in an airtight container in the refrigerator for up to 3 days. Reheat in the oven at 350°F (180°C) for 7 to 10 minutes or until warmed through.

LE CREUSET
LE CREUSET

Stuffed Shells

These stuffed shells have been one of my favorite dishes to make for as long as I can remember. They're cheesy, comforting, and always a hit at the dinner table. I never imagined that when I shared this recipe online, it would take off the way it did—more than 26 million people have watched me make these! It's proof that sometimes the most classic dishes are the ones that bring the most joy.

Prep Time:	Cook Time:	Total Time:	Serves:
30 minutes	1 hour, 25 minutes	1 hour, 55 minutes	6–8

Equipment

Knife
Cutting board
Large pot
Colander
Large skillet
Wooden spoon
Medium skillet
Large mixing bowl
9 × 13-inch (23 × 33cm) baking dish
Aluminum foil

Ingredients

12 oz (340g) package jumbo pasta shells
2 tbsp extra-virgin olive oil, divided
1 small yellow onion, diced
4 cups tomato sauce
1 tsp salt, plus a pinch to taste
½ tsp freshly ground black pepper, plus a pinch to taste
2 garlic cloves, minced
4 cups fresh spinach, chopped
2 cups ricotta
2 cups shredded mozzarella
½ cup grated Parmesan, plus more for topping
2 large eggs
2 tbsp chopped fresh parsley
Fresh basil leaves, for garnish (optional)

1. Preheat the oven to 375°F (190°C).
2. Bring a large pot of salted water to a boil over high heat. Add the jumbo pasta shells, and cook until al dente, according to the package instructions. Drain the pasta and set aside to cool slightly.
3. Heat 1 tablespoon olive oil in a large skillet over medium heat. Add the diced onions, and cook until softened and lightly browned, about 5 minutes.
4. Pour in the tomato sauce, season with a pinch of salt and pepper, and simmer, stirring occasionally, for about 20 minutes.
5. Meanwhile, heat the remaining 1 tablespoon olive oil in a medium skillet over medium heat. Add the minced garlic, and sauté until fragrant, about 30 seconds.
6. Stir in the spinach, season with another pinch of salt and pepper, and cook until wilted, 2 to 3 minutes. Remove from the heat, and let it cool slightly.
7. Transfer the spinach to a large mixing bowl. Add the ricotta, mozzarella, Parmesan, eggs, parsley, the remaining 1 teaspoon salt, and the remaining ½ teaspoon pepper, and stir until well combined.
8. Spread 1 cup marinara sauce evenly in the bottom of a 9 × 13-inch (23 × 33cm) baking dish.
9. Fill each pasta shell with a generous spoonful of the cheese mixture. Arrange the stuffed shells in a single layer in the baking dish and then pour the remaining marinara sauce over top, ensuring all shells are well covered. Sprinkle with more grated Parmesan cheese.
10. Cover with aluminum foil, and bake for 30 minutes. Uncover and bake for 15 more minutes, or until the cheese is bubbly and golden. Garnish with fresh basil leaves (if using).
11. Serve hot. Store leftovers in an airtight container in the refrigerator for up to 3 days. Reheat in the oven at 350°F (180°C) for 10 to 12 minutes or until warmed through.

Pork Braciole

When I was growing up, Sundays were always special in our home. The aroma of pork braciole simmering in tomato sauce would fill the house, signaling a day of family, laughter, and, of course, delicious food. This dish embodies the warmth and love of those cherished family gatherings, which I often look back on with a smile. This recipe has been passed down in my family through generations, and I'm delighted to share it with you. Serve it with pasta or Italian bread for a hearty, comforting meal.

PREP TIME:	COOK TIME:	TOTAL TIME:	SERVES:
20 MINUTES	ABOUT 2 HOURS	ABOUT 2½ HOURS	4–6

Equipment

Knife
Cutting board
Plastic wrap
Meat mallet
Toothpicks or kitchen twine
Large skillet with lid
Wooden spoon

Ingredients

- 8 thin slices pork shoulder (about 4 ounces per slice)
- 4 garlic cloves, minced
- ¼ cup fresh Italian parsley, whole leaves
- ¼ cup grated Pecorino Romano, plus more for garnish
- 1 tsp salt, plus more to taste
- ½ tsp freshly ground black pepper, plus more to taste
- 2 tbsp olive oil
- 1 large yellow onion, finely chopped
- ½ cup dry white wine
- 28 oz (800g) can crushed tomatoes
- 8 fresh basil leaves, plus more for garnish

1. Place each slice of pork shoulder between two sheets of plastic wrap. Using a meat mallet, gently pound the pork to an even thickness of ¼ inch (6mm).
2. Lay each pork slice flat on a clean workspace. Evenly distribute the garlic, parsley, Pecorino Romano, salt, and pepper among the pork slices.
3. To make the braciole, starting from one end, roll the pork slices tightly into a cylinder over the filling. Secure each roll with toothpicks or kitchen twine (if you want to be like Nonna) to prevent them from unrolling while cooking.
4. Heat the olive oil in a large skillet over medium-high heat. Add the onion and braciole, and brown the braciole on all sides, 2 to 3 minutes per side.
5. Pour in the white wine to deglaze the pan, scraping up any browned bits from the bottom. Let the wine reduce by half, about 5 minutes.
6. Pour the crushed tomatoes over the braciole, ensuring they are fully submerged. Add the fresh basil and more salt and pepper, and stir gently to combine. Bring the sauce to a simmer and then reduce the heat to low. Cover the skillet and let the braciole cook slowly, uncovering and stirring occasionally to prevent sticking, until the pork is tender and the flavors have melded, 1½ to 2 hours.
7. When the braciole is cooked, remove the toothpicks or twine.
8. Serve the braciole hot, topped with the rich tomato sauce and alongside pasta or Italian bread. Garnish with additional fresh basil leaves and more grated Pecorino Romano. Store leftovers in an airtight container in the refrigerator for up to 3 days. Reheat gently in a medium frying pan over medium-low heat for 12 to 15 minutes.

Nonna's Sunday Sauce

Notice I didn't call this "Nonna's Sunday *Gravy*." It's sauce, because gravy is what you pour over the Thanksgiving turkey. Anyway, this Sunday sauce recipe is more than just a meal—it's part of the fabric we Italians are made of. Slow cooked with a mix of meats, onions, and a rich tomato-sauce base, this is the heart and soul of Sunday dinner. My version is made with Italian sausage, pork ribs, and pork braciole, all simmered to perfection. If you want to spice things up, feel free to use my Pork Braciole (page 92) to make your own and add it to the sauce.

Equipment

Knife
Cutting board
Large pot
Wooden spoon

Ingredients

3 tbsp extra-virgin olive oil
1 lb (450g) Italian sausage
1 lb (450g) pork ribs
1 lb (450g) Pork Braciole (page 92)
1 medium yellow onion, sliced
½ cup dry white wine
72 oz (2kg) crushed plum tomatoes
1½ tsp kosher salt
½ tsp freshly ground black pepper
¼ cup fresh basil

Prep time:	Cook time:	Total time:	Serves:
15 minutes	2 hours, 15 minutes	2 hours, 30 minutes	6–8

1. Heat the olive oil in a large pot over medium heat. Add the Italian sausage, pork ribs, and pork braciole, and sauté until the meat is golden brown on all sides, about 2 to 3 minutes per side.
2. Add the sliced onion, and sauté until softened, about 3 minutes.
3. Pour in the white wine and let it cook off for a few minutes, stirring occasionally.
4. Add the crushed plum tomatoes, salt, pepper, and basil, and stir to combine. Reduce the heat to low, and let the sauce simmer, stirring occasionally, for 2 hours.
5. Serve hot over your favorite pasta. Store leftovers in an airtight container in the refrigerator for up to 3 days. Reheat gently in a large frying pan over medium-low heat for about 15 minutes.

Linguine with Blue Crab Tomato Sauce

Equipment

Knife
Cutting board
Large heavy-bottomed pot with lid
Wooden spoon
Large pot
Colander
Tongs

Ingredients

- ¼ cup extra-virgin olive oil, plus more for garnish
- 4 garlic cloves, smashed
- 72 oz (2kg) crushed plum tomatoes (about 3 large cans), with juice
- ¼ cup fresh basil leaves
- Kosher salt to taste
- Freshly ground black pepper to taste
- 8 whole blue crabs, cleaned and halved
- 2 lb (1kg) linguine pasta
- Pinch of crushed red pepper flakes (optional)
- Chopped fresh parsley (optional)

We didn't have blue crab in Sarno, but after I moved to America, it became one of my favorite flavors to add to a fresh tomato sauce. I remember walking down Arthur Avenue in the Bronx and always stopping at Randazzo's Seafood, my local fish market, picking up some blue crabs from a crate in front of the shop, going home, and getting straight to work. I made this dish on special occasions, especially when the crabs were fresh and sweet. The aroma of the sauce simmering with the crabs is among the best scents you can experience. This dish is messy to eat (so have napkins at the ready!), but it's worth every bite.

Prep Time:	Cook Time:	Total Time:	Serves:
20 minutes	2 hours, 15 minutes	2 hours, 35 minutes	6–8

1. Heat a large heavy-bottomed pot over medium heat, and add the olive oil. When the oil is hot, add the garlic and sauté until fragrant but not browned, 1 or 2 minutes.
2. Carefully pour in the crushed plum tomatoes, stir in the basil leaves, and season with salt and pepper. Let the sauce come to a gentle simmer and then reduce the heat to low.
3. Nestle the blue crabs in the sauce and then partially cover with a lid and simmer gently, stirring occasionally, for about 2 hours. The crabs will turn bright red and infuse the sauce with their briny sweetness.
4. About 15 minutes before the sauce is done, bring a large pot of salted water to a boil over high heat. Cook the linguine until just al dente, according to package instructions. Reserve about ½ cup of the pasta water before draining the pasta.
5. Add the crushed red pepper flakes (if using, for a little heat) to the sauce.
6. Remove the pot from the heat, and toss the pasta in the sauce, adding a bit of the reserved pasta water as needed for consistency. Stir to coat well.
7. Serve the pasta topped with the crabs, a drizzle of good olive oil (Nonna's Olive Oil is best!), and fresh parsley (if using). Store the leftover sauce and crab separate from the pasta in airtight containers in the refrigerator for up to 2 days. Reheat gently in a medium frying pan over medium heat for 7 to 10 minutes.

Spaghettini alle Vongole

This dish is one of my favorites because it's quick, fresh, and packed with flavor. The key is using really good extra-virgin olive oil, like Nonna's Olive Oil—trust me, it makes all the difference! As you watch the clams open in the pan, you know you're in for something special.

Prep Time:	Cook Time:	Total Time:	Serves:
15 minutes	20 minutes	35 minutes	4

Equipment

Knife
Cutting board
Large mixing bowl
Deep skillet
Wooden spoon
Large pot
Colander

Ingredients

2 lb (450g) small vongole clams
6 tbsp extra-virgin olive oil, plus more for garnish
4 garlic cloves, sliced
1 cup clam juice
¼ cup roughly chopped fresh parsley
1 tsp salt
½ tsp freshly ground black pepper
½ tsp crushed red pepper flakes
1 lb (450g) spaghettini pasta

1. Add the clams to a large mixing bowl, and rinse them under running water, repeating 3 to 5 times until no sand remains. Set aside.
2. Heat the olive oil in a deep skillet over medium heat. Add the sliced garlic, and cook until golden brown, about 1 to 2 minutes.
3. Add the clams, clam juice, parsley, salt, pepper, and crushed red pepper flakes. Stir gently and cook until the clams open, 7 to 10 minutes.
4. Meanwhile, bring a large pot of salted water to a boil over high heat. Add the spaghettini and cook until al dente, according to package instructions. Drain the pasta.
5. Add the pasta to the skillet with the clams. Toss everything together, allowing the pasta to absorb the flavors of the sauce.
6. Serve hot, with an extra drizzle of your favorite olive oil. Store leftovers in an airtight container in the refrigerator for up to 1 day. Reheat gently in a pan over medium heat for 5 to 7 minutes, adding a splash of water or olive oil.

Penne Puttanesca

This is one of those dishes that comes together quickly but is packed with bold flavors. The combination of olives, capers, and garlic makes for a rich and savory sauce that pairs perfectly with al dente pasta.

Prep Time:	Cook Time:	Total Time:	Serves:
10 minutes	35 minutes	45 minutes	4–6

Equipment

Knife
Cutting board
Large skillet
Wooden spoon
Large pot
Colander

Ingredients

4 tbsp extra-virgin olive oil
4 garlic cloves, sliced
½ cup kalamata olives, pitted
2 tbsp capers
3 cups tomato purée (passata di pomodoro)
1 tsp salt
½ tsp freshly ground black pepper
¼ cup fresh basil, whole
1 lb (450g) penne pasta
Grated Pecorino Romano, for garnish

1. Heat the olive oil in a large skillet over medium heat. Add the sliced garlic, and cook until golden brown, about 1 to 2 minutes.
2. Add the olives and capers, stir to combine, and cook for about 2 minutes.
3. Pour in the tomato purée and then add the salt, pepper, and basil. Stir well and simmer the sauce, stirring occasionally, for 30 minutes.
4. Meanwhile, bring a large pot of salted water to a boil over high heat. Add the penne and cook until al dente, according to package instructions. Drain the pasta.
5. Add the pasta to the skillet with the sauce, and toss well to coat.
6. Serve hot with grated Pecorino Romano sprinkled on top. Store leftovers in an airtight container in the refrigerator for up to 2 days. Reheat with a splash of water or olive oil in a medium frying pan over medium heat for 5 to 7 minutes.

Baked Rigatoni alla Norma

This dish brings back memories of cozy Sunday nights, when the scent of roasted eggplant and simmering sauce would fill the whole house. The recipe is a southern Italian classic, and it's comforting, flavorful, and deeply satisfying. The smoky mozzarella melts into the rigatoni, the eggplant soaks up all the rich tomato goodness, and the crispy top gives it the perfect finish. It's a meal that reminds me how the simplest ingredients, when treated with love, can make the most memorable dishes.

PREP TIME:	COOK TIME:	TOTAL TIME:	SERVES:
15 MINUTES	1 HOUR	1 HOUR, 15 MINUTES	6

Equipment

Knife
Cutting board
Large skillet
Baking sheet
Large pot
Colander
Wooden spoon
9 × 13-inch (23 × 33cm) baking dish

Ingredients

- ¼ cup extra-virgin olive oil, plus more for drizzling and serving
- 3 garlic cloves, peeled
- 5 cups tomato purée (passata di pomodoro)
- A few fresh basil leaves
- Kosher salt to taste
- Freshly ground black pepper to taste
- 1 medium eggplant, diced (about 1 lb/450g)
- ½ tsp garlic powder
- 1 lb (450g) rigatoni pasta
- 1 cup smoked mozzarella, diced
- ½ cup grated Parmigiano-Reggiano, plus more for serving

1. Heat a large skillet over medium heat, and add the olive oil. When the oil is hot, add the garlic and sauté until golden brown, 2 to 3 minutes. You can remove and discard the garlic now or leave it in for a stronger flavor.
2. Add the tomato purée and basil, and season with salt and pepper. Reduce the heat to low, and let the sauce simmer for 20 minutes.
3. Meanwhile, preheat the oven to 400°F (200°C).
4. Place the diced eggplant on a baking sheet. Drizzle with olive oil, add the garlic powder, and season with salt and pepper. Toss well to evenly coat.
5. Roast for 25 to 30 minutes, until tender and golden.
6. While the eggplant is roasting, bring a large pot of salted water to a boil over high heat. Cook the rigatoni according to package instructions until al dente. Drain and set aside.
7. Add the roasted eggplant to the tomato sauce and stir. Let everything cook together for 5 more minutes so the eggplant can absorb the flavors.
8. Remove from the heat and add the rigatoni. Stir in the smoked mozzarella and grated Parmigiano-Reggiano until evenly combined. Transfer to a 9 × 13-inch (23 × 33cm) baking dish.
9. Bake for 30 minutes, or until the top is golden and crispy.
10. Serve hot, drizzled with a little olive oil and a sprinkle of grated Parmigiano-Reggiano. Store leftovers in an airtight container in the refrigerator for up to 3 days. Reheat in the oven at 375°F (190°C) for 10 to 15 minutes.

Bucatini All'Amatriciana

This dish is a Roman cuisine classic, known for its rich, savory flavors and simple ingredients that come together beautifully. I have been making this recipe for as long as I can remember, and it has always been one of my favorites. The key to a perfect bucatini all'amatriciana is using high-quality ingredients—good pancetta, fresh tomatoes, and plenty of Parmigiano-Reggiano. Like most of the recipes in this cookbook, it's a dish that proves that sometimes the simplest recipes taste the best.

PREP TIME:	COOK TIME:	TOTAL TIME:	SERVES:
10 MINUTES	30 MINUTES	40 MINUTES	4

Equipment

Knife
Cutting board
Large skillet
Wooden spoon
Large pot
Colander
Tongs

Ingredients

- 8 oz (225g) pancetta, cut into small pieces
- 1 small yellow onion, diced
- 2 cups grape tomatoes, halved
- 1 lb (450g) bucatini pasta
- Salt and freshly ground black pepper to taste
- 2/3 cup grated Parmigiano-Reggiano, divided

1. Heat a large skillet over low heat. Add the pancetta and cook slowly, rendering the fat, about 5 minutes.
2. When the pancetta is about halfway cooked, add the diced onion. Cook, stirring occasionally, until the onion is softened and lightly golden, about 5 minutes.
3. Add the grape tomatoes and stir to combine. Increase the heat to medium, and cook the sauce, stirring occasionally, for about 20 minutes.
4. Meanwhile, bring a large pot of salted water to a boil over high heat. Add the bucatini and cook until just shy of al dente, according to the package instructions.
5. When the pasta is nearly al dente, ladle ½ cup of the pasta water into the sauce. Stir to combine, and season with salt and pepper.
6. Drain the pasta, add it to the sauce, and toss well to coat the pasta. Cook for 1 or 2 minutes so the pasta can absorb the flavors of the sauce.
7. Remove from the heat and stir in half of the grated Parmigiano-Reggiano.
8. To serve, use tongs to divide the pasta among four plates and top with the remaining Parmigiano-Reggiano. Store leftovers in an airtight container in the refrigerator for up to 3 days. Reheat in a skillet with olive oil over medium heat for 5 to 7 minutes.

Tagliatelle Bolognese

Bolognese sauce is one of those dishes that takes time, but the results are always worth it. Slow cooked with a mixture of ground beef and veal, white wine, and a rich tomato base, the sauce coats the tagliatelle beautifully. Served with extra sauce and plenty of grated cheese, this is a dish that brings everyone to the table.

Prep time:	Cook time:	Total time:	Serves:
15 minutes	1 hour, 10 minutes	1 hour, 25 minutes	4–6

Equipment

Knife
Cutting board
Large skillet
Wooden spoon
Large pot
Colander

Ingredients

4 tbsp extra-virgin olive oil
1 small yellow onion, chopped
1 small carrot, peeled and chopped
1 celery stalk, chopped
1 lb (450g) ground beef-and-veal mix
½ cup dry white wine
4 cups tomato purée (passata di pomodoro)
1½ tsp salt
½ tsp freshly ground black pepper
¼ cup fresh basil
1 lb (450g) tagliatelle pasta
Grated Pecorino Romano, for garnish

1. Heat the olive oil in a large skillet over medium heat. Add the onion, carrot, and celery, and sauté until softened, about 5 to 6 minutes.
2. Add the ground beef and veal, and cook, breaking up the meats with a wooden spoon until fully browned, about 5 minutes.
3. Pour in the white wine and let it cook down, allowing the alcohol to evaporate.
4. Stir in the tomato purée, season with the salt and pepper, and add the basil. Stir well. Reduce the heat to low, and simmer, stirring occasionally, for about 1 hour.
5. When the sauce is almost done, bring a large pot of salted water to a boil over high heat. Cook the tagliatelle until al dente, according to package instructions. Drain the pasta.
6. Add the pasta to the skillet with the Bolognese sauce, and toss well to coat.
7. Serve hot in bowls with extra sauce and a generous sprinkle of grated Pecorino Romano. Store leftovers in an airtight container in the refrigerator for up to 3 days. Reheat gently in a medium frying pan over medium heat for 5 to 7 minutes, adding a splash of water.

Risotto alla Pescatora
(Seafood Risotto)

If there was ever a dish that tasted like the greatest treasures of the sea, this is it. My Risotto alla Pescatora is all about layering delicate seafood flavors, one ladle at a time, until every grain of rice is infused with richness. The trick is patience—and ensuring you don't rush the rice. This isn't something you throw together. You stand by the stove, stirring the rice, maybe sipping a little wine, and letting the risotto tell you when it's ready.

Prep Time:	Cook Time:	Total Time:	Serves:
30 minutes	40 minutes	1 hour, 10 minutes	6

Equipment

Knife
Cutting board
Medium saucepan (to heat the stock)
Large saucepan with lid
Fine-mesh sieve
Large, wide-bottomed pan
Wooden spoon
Ladle

Ingredients

2 dozen littleneck clams, scrubbed
2 dozen mussels, scrubbed and debearded
½ cup dry white wine, plus more for steaming
¼ cup extra-virgin olive oil
1 medium yellow onion, finely diced
2 cups Carnaroli rice or Arborio rice
4 cups hot seafood stock, plus more as needed
Kosher salt to taste
Freshly ground black pepper to taste
8 oz (225g) cooked lobster meat, cut into chunks
8 oz (225g) shrimp, peeled and deveined
2 tbsp chopped fresh parsley

1. Add the clams and mussels to a large saucepan along with a splash of white wine and a few tablespoons of water. Cover with a lid, set over medium heat, and steam until the shells open, 5 to 7 minutes. Transfer the shellfish to a bowl, and discard any that remain closed. Remove the meat from the shells and set aside. Strain the steaming liquid through a fine-mesh sieve, and add it to the hot seafood stock.
2. Heat the olive oil in a large, wide-bottomed pan over low heat. When the oil is hot, add the onion and sauté until soft and translucent, 2 to 3 minutes. Be careful not to let the onion brown.
3. Increase the heat to medium, and add the rice. Cook, stirring continuously, for 2 to 3 minutes, allowing the rice to toast slightly and absorb the oil.
4. Pour in the remaining ½ cup white wine, and stir until the wine is mostly absorbed, 2 to 4 minutes.
5. Add the hot seafood stock, one ladleful at a time, stirring constantly between additions. Allow the liquid to be mostly absorbed before adding more. When you've added about half of the stock, season the rice with salt and pepper. Continue adding the hot stock until the rice is al dente, 20 to 25 minutes.
6. When the rice is just shy of being done, stir in the lobster meat and continue cooking for 2 to 3 minutes. Then add the shrimp and cook until they are just cooked through, 3 to 4 minutes.
7. Gently stir in the shelled clams and mussels, and cook until just warmed through, 1 to 2 minutes.
8. Remove the skillet from the heat, sprinkle with the fresh parsley, and let the risotto rest for 1 minute.
9. Serve hot, ideally with a glass of crisp white wine. Risotto is best enjoyed right away, but leftovers can be stored in an airtight container in the refrigerator for up to 2 days. Reheat gently in a medium frying pan over medium heat for 5 to 7 minutes, adding a splash of stock or water.

Risotto ai Funghi

(Mushroom Risotto)

There's something magical about the smell of mushrooms and onions sizzling in olive oil. This risotto ai funghi is one of those comforting dishes that feels fancy but comes from humble ingredients. When porcini mushrooms are in season, I don't pass up on the opportunity to use them in this recipe. Their earthy flavor melts into every grain of rice, and with the help of some good stock and a little patience, you get something that warms the soul.

Prep Time:	Cook Time:	Total Time:	Serves:
15 minutes	45 minutes	1 hour	6

Equipment

Knife
Cutting board
Medium saucepan (to heat the stock)
Large, wide-bottomed pan
Wooden spoon
Ladle

Ingredients

¼ cup extra-virgin olive oil
1 medium yellow onion, finely diced
8 oz (225g) porcini mushrooms, chopped
2 cups Carnaroli rice or Arborio rice
½ cup dry white wine
5–6 cups hot vegetable stock
Kosher salt to taste
Freshly ground black pepper to taste
1 stick unsalted butter, cut into pieces
1 cup grated Parmigiano-Reggiano, plus more for serving (optional)

1. Heat the olive oil in a large, wide-bottomed pan over low heat. When the oil is hot, add the onion and porcini mushrooms. Cook, stirring occasionally, until the onions are soft and translucent and the mushrooms are fragrant and tender, about 8 minutes. Be careful not to let the onions brown.
2. Increase the heat to medium, and add the rice. Cook, stirring continuously, until the grains are lightly toasted and well coated in the oil, 2 or 3 minutes.
3. Pour in the white wine and stir until the wine has mostly evaporated, 2 to 4 minutes.
4. Add the hot vegetable stock, one ladleful at a time, stirring constantly between additions. Allow the liquid to be mostly absorbed before adding more. When you've added about half of the stock, season the rice with salt and pepper. Continue adding the hot stock until the rice is al dente, 20 to 25 minutes.
5. When the rice is just shy of being done, reduce the heat to low, add the butter, and stir until melted.
6. Add the grated Parmigiano-Reggiano, and mix until creamy and well combined.
7. Remove the skillet from the heat, and let the risotto rest for 1 minute.
8. Serve hot, with extra grated Parmigiano-Reggiano on top (if using). Risotto is best enjoyed right away, but leftovers can be stored in an airtight container in the refrigerator for up to 2 days. Reheat gently in a medium frying pan over medium heat for 5 to 7 minutes, adding a splash of stock or water.

Risotto alla Milanesa

This risotto might look basic, but don't let that fool you—it's rich, elegant, and full of soul. I've made this dish more times than I can count, and I always say the same thing: When you use the right ingredients and take your time, even dishes this simple can become something special. The aroma of saffron, the creaminess of the rice, and that final swirl of butter and cheese ... it's like a warm hug from the inside.

Prep Time:	Cook Time:	Total Time:	Serves:
10 minutes	30 minutes	40 minutes	4

Equipment

Knife
Cutting board
Medium saucepan (to heat the stock)
Large, wide-bottomed pan
Wooden spoon
Ladle

Ingredients

¼ cup extra-virgin olive oil
1 small yellow onion, finely diced
2 cups Carnaroli rice or Arborio rice
½ cup dry white wine
4–5 cups hot chicken stock, plus more as needed
Pinch of saffron threads
Kosher salt to taste
Freshly ground black pepper to taste
1 stick of unsalted butter, cut into pieces
1 cup grated Parmigiano-Reggiano, plus more for serving (optional)

1. Heat the olive oil in a large, wide-bottomed pan over low heat. When the oil is hot, add the onion and sauté gently until soft and translucent, 2 to 3 minutes. Be careful not to let it brown.
2. Add the rice, increase the heat to medium, and cook, stirring continuously, for 2 to 3 minutes, letting the grains toast slightly and absorb the oil.
3. Pour in the white wine, and stir until it is mostly absorbed by the rice.
4. Add the hot chicken stock, one ladleful at a time, stirring constantly between additions. Allow the liquid to be mostly absorbed before adding more. Early in this process, stir in the saffron threads and season with salt and pepper to taste. Continue adding the hot stock until the rice is tender but still has a slight bite, 20 to 25 minutes.
5. When the rice is just shy of being done, reduce the heat to low, add the butter, and stir until melted.
6. Fold in the grated Parmigiano-Reggiano. Taste and adjust the seasonings to your liking.
7. Remove the pan from the heat, and let the risotto rest for 1 minute.
8. Serve hot, with a little extra grated Parmigiano-Reggiano on top (if using). Risotto is best enjoyed right away, but leftovers can be stored in an airtight container in the refrigerator for up to 2 days. Reheat gently in a medium frying pan over medium heat for 5 to 7 minutes, adding a splash of stock or water.

Secondi Piatti

(The Main Course)

Cutlets

Thin, crispy, and perfectly golden brown, these cutlets are always a hit in my house. Whether made with chicken or veal, the key to success is pounding them until they're nice and thin. These cutlets are simple but packed with flavor, thanks to a well-seasoned breadcrumb coating and a final sprinkle of flaky sea salt.

Prep Time:	Cook Time:	Total Time:	Serves:
15 minutes	10 minutes	25 minutes	2

Equipment

Plastic wrap
Meat mallet
Whisk
2 shallow bowls
Large skillet
Tongs
Paper towels
Plate

Ingredients

4 thin chicken or veal cutlets
2 large eggs
1½ tsp salt, or to taste, divided
¾ tsp freshly ground black pepper, divided
1½ cups plain breadcrumbs
¼ cup grated Pecorino Romano
½ tsp dried parsley flakes
½ tsp dried basil
½ tsp dried oregano
½ tsp garlic powder
½ tsp onion powder
1 cup vegetable oil
Flaky sea salt, for garnish
Lemon wedges, for garnish

1. Place the cutlets between two sheets of plastic wrap. Using a meat mallet, gently pound the cutlets to an even thickness of ¼ inch (6mm).
2. Beat the eggs in one shallow bowl. Season with 1 teaspoon salt and ½ teaspoon pepper.
3. Add the breadcrumbs, the remaining ½ teaspoon salt, remaining ¼ teaspoon pepper, Pecorino Romano, parsley flakes, basil, oregano, garlic powder, and onion powder to another shallow bowl. Mix well.
4. Dip each cutlet into the egg mixture, ensuring it's fully coated. Then, press it firmly into the seasoned breadcrumbs, covering all sides evenly.
5. Heat the vegetable oil in a large skillet over medium-high heat until it reaches 350°F (180°C). Fry the cutlets in batches until golden brown and crispy, 2 or 3 minutes per side. Using tongs, transfer the cutlets to a paper towel–lined plate to drain the excess oil.
6. Sprinkle each cutlet with a pinch of flaky sea salt.
7. Serve immediately with lemon wedges on the side. Store leftovers in an airtight container in the refrigerator for up to 2 days. Reheat in the oven on a medium baking sheet at 375°F (190°C) for 10 minutes to maintain crispiness.

Chicken Marsala

Equipment

Knife
Cutting board
Plastic wrap
Meat mallet
Shallow bowl
Large skillet
Plate
Wooden spoon

Ingredients

4 boneless, skinless chicken breasts
1 tsp salt, divided
½ tsp freshly ground black pepper, divided
1 cup all-purpose flour
9 tbsp extra-virgin olive oil, divided
2 tbsp unsalted butter
2 shallots, finely chopped
8 oz (225g) cremini mushrooms, sliced
¾ cup dry marsala wine
¾ cup chicken broth
2 tbsp chopped fresh parsley

This classic Italian American dish features tender chicken cutlets simmered in a rich marsala wine sauce with mushrooms and shallots. It's a comforting meal that's perfect for family dinners or special occasions.

Prep Time:	Cook Time:	Total Time:	Serves:
15 minutes	20 minutes	35 minutes	4

1. Place the chicken between two sheets of plastic wrap. Using a meat mallet, gently pound the chicken to an even thickness of ½ inch (1.25cm).
2. Season both sides of the chicken with ½ teaspoon salt and ¼ teaspoon pepper.
3. Place the flour in a shallow bowl. Dredge each chicken breast in the flour, shaking off any excess.
4. Heat 7 tablespoons olive oil in a large skillet over medium-high heat. Add the chicken and cook until golden brown on both sides, 3 or 4 minutes per side. Transfer the chicken to a plate and set aside.
5. Remove about half of the leftover oil in the skillet and discard. Reduce the heat to medium, and add the butter. When the butter has melted, add the shallots and cook until translucent, about 2 minutes.
6. Add the cremini mushrooms, and cook until browned, about 5 minutes.
7. Pour in the dry marsala wine, scraping up any browned bits from the bottom of the skillet. Simmer for about 2 minutes to reduce slightly.
8. Pour in the chicken broth, the remaining 2 tablespoons olive oil, the remaining ½ teaspoon of salt, and remaining ¼ teaspoon of pepper. Bring the mixture to a simmer.
9. Return the chicken to the skillet, spooning some of the sauce over it. Let the chicken cook in the sauce until the chicken is cooked through and the sauce has thickened slightly, about 5 minutes.
10. Sprinkle with the chopped fresh parsley, and serve warm, topped with the mushroom sauce. Store leftovers in an airtight container in the refrigerator for up to 3 days. Reheat gently in a medium frying pan over medium heat for 2 to 3 minutes.

Chicken Francese

I learned most of my recipes in Italy from my mother, and I still cook plenty of traditional Italian dishes, but living in New York has opened my eyes to so many new flavors, and this dish is a perfect example of how my cooking has evolved. When I moved to New York, my husband, John, worked in a Manhattan restaurant that served all the classic New York Italian dishes—things I had never seen back home. One of his favorites was chicken Francese. He loved it so much that he asked the chef to teach him how to make it, and before long, John had it perfected. One day he taught me, and I've been making it ever since.

Prep time:	Cook time:	Total time:	Serves:
10 minutes	15 minutes	25 minutes	2

Equipment

Knife
Cutting board
Plastic wrap
Meat mallet
Whisk
2 shallow bowls
Large skillet
Wire rack
Wooden spoon

Ingredients

- 6 thin-sliced chicken cutlets
- 3 large eggs
- Salt and freshly ground black pepper to taste
- 1 cup all-purpose flour
- ¾ cup (175ml) vegetable oil
- ½ cup (120ml) dry white wine (such as pinot grigio or sauvignon blanc)
- 2 tbsp unsalted butter
- 1 cup chicken stock
- Juice of ½ lemon
- 2 tbsp finely chopped fresh parsley, for garnish
- 1 lemon, sliced into wedges, for garnish

1. Place the chicken cutlets between two sheets of plastic wrap. Using a meat mallet, gently pound the chicken to an even thickness of ¼ inch (6mm).
2. Whisk the eggs in one shallow bowl, and season with salt and pepper to taste.
3. Add the flour to another shallow bowl.
4. Heat the vegetable oil in a large skillet over medium heat until shimmering.
5. Working in batches, coat each chicken cutlet in flour, shaking off any excess, and then dip it into the egg mixture, ensuring an even coating. Add the chicken to the skillet and fry until golden brown, about 3 minutes per side. Transfer to a wire rack or paper towel-lined plate, and set aside.
6. Discard the oil in the skillet, leaving behind any browned bits, and return the skillet to medium heat. Add the white wine, butter, chicken stock, and lemon juice, and simmer for 3 to 5 minutes, to allow the alcohol to cook off.
7. Return the chicken to the skillet, and spoon the sauce over each cutlet. Let the chicken simmer for 3 to 5 minutes to ensure it's fully cooked and infused with the sauce. If the sauce thickens too much, add more chicken stock or water to loosen it.
8. Sprinkle with the chopped parsley, and serve with the lemon wedges on the side. Store leftovers in an airtight container in the refrigerator for up to 3 days. Reheat gently in a skillet over medium heat for 5 to 7 minutes.

Chicken Scarpariello

Some people say this dish isn't truly Italian, but I say it's truly delicious. I didn't grow up eating chicken scarpariello in Sarno—it's one of those Italian American recipes that took on a life of its own in kitchens across New York—but I made it plenty of times after moving to the States. I was born in Italy, yet I have spent most of my life in America, so I find myself at home in both worlds. This dish has a little bit of sweetness, a little heat, and a lot of flavor. It might not be traditional, but it feels like home to me.

Prep time:	Cook time:	Total time:	Serves:
20 minutes	40 minutes	1 hour	4–6

Equipment

Knife
Cutting board
Shallow bowl
Large skillet
Large mixing bowl
Paper towels
Wooden spoon

Ingredients

½ cup all-purpose flour
1½ lb (680g) boneless, skinless chicken breasts, cut into chunks
Kosher salt to taste
Freshly ground black pepper to taste
½ cup vegetable oil
8 sweet Italian sausages, casings removed
4 garlic cloves, minced
1 cup sliced red, yellow, or orange sweet bell peppers
2–3 pickled cherry peppers, sliced, or to taste
1 cup dry white wine
Juice of ½ lemon
1 tbsp unsalted butter
1 cube of chicken bouillon
Chopped fresh parsley, for garnish

1 Place the flour in a shallow bowl.

2 Season the chicken with salt and pepper and then dredge it lightly in the flour, shaking off any excess.

3 Heat a large skillet over medium-high heat, and add the vegetable oil. When the oil is hot, and working in batches, fry the chicken until golden brown all over, 2 or 3 minutes per side. (The chicken does not need to be fully cooked at this stage.) Transfer the chicken to a large mixing bowl lined with paper towels to absorb the excess oil. Set aside.

4 Add the sausage meat to the same skillet, reduce the heat to medium, and cook, breaking up the sausage with a wooden spoon, until browned and just cooked through, 3 to 5 minutes.

5 Return the chicken to the skillet. Add the garlic, bell peppers, and cherry peppers; stir; and cook for 2 or 3 minutes.

6 Pour in the white wine, and simmer for 2 minutes.

7 Add the lemon juice, butter, bouillon, and 1 cup water, and stir to combine. Reduce the heat to low, and simmer until the chicken is fully cooked and the sauce has slightly thickened, 15 to 20 minutes.

8 Sprinkle with the chopped parsley and serve hot, preferably with some crunchy bread or roasted potatoes. Store leftovers in an airtight container in the refrigerator for up to 3 days. Reheat gently in a medium frying pan over medium heat for 5 to 7 minutes.

Chicken Cacciatore

When I was growing up in post–World War II Sarno, chicken wasn't as readily available as it is today in the United States. So whenever we had it and my mother made chicken cacciatore, it was a special meal for the whole family. This dish is hearty, full of flavor, and made with simple ingredients that come together beautifully.

Prep time:	Cook time:	Total time:	Serves:
15 minutes	1 hour, 5 minutes	1 hour, 20 minutes	4

Equipment

Knife
Cutting board
Large skillet
Wooden spoon

Ingredients

- 4 tbsp extra-virgin olive oil
- 4 garlic cloves
- 6 bone-in, skin-on chicken thighs and drumsticks, patted dry
- 1 tsp salt
- ½ tsp freshly ground black pepper
- ½ tsp crushed red pepper flakes
- ½ cup dry white wine
- 4 plum tomatoes, crushed
- 1 cup sliced white button mushrooms
- 1 large red bell pepper, ribs and seeds removed, and sliced
- 1 small white onion, sliced
- ¼ cup chopped fresh parsley

1. Heat the olive oil in a large skillet over medium heat. Add the garlic cloves, and cook until golden brown, about 2 minutes.
2. Add the chicken thighs and drumsticks, and season with the salt, pepper, and crushed red pepper flakes. Let the chicken brown for about 4 to 6 minutes per side.
3. Pour in the white wine, and allow it to cook down and absorb into the chicken, about 3 minutes.
4. When the chicken is almost cooked through, add the crushed plum tomatoes, mushrooms, bell pepper, onion, and parsley. Stir well to combine, and simmer until the vegetables are tender and the chicken is fully cooked, about 10 minutes.
5. Serve hot, preferably with fresh bread. Store leftovers in an airtight container in the refrigerator for up to 3 days. Reheat in a large frying pan over low heat for 8 to 10 minutes or until warmed through.

Veal Milanese

There's nothing better than a perfectly crispy veal Milanese. I've been making this dish for years. A crunchy golden crust, a sprinkle of flaky sea salt, and a bright lemon wedge on the side—it's a meal that never fails to impress. I like to serve it with a fresh tomato and arugula salad, simply dressed with extra-virgin olive oil.

Prep Time:	Cook Time:	Total Time:	Serves:
15 minutes	10 minutes	25 minutes	4

Equipment

Knife
Cutting board
Plastic wrap
Meat mallet
Whisk
2 shallow bowls
Large skillet
Tongs
Paper towels
Plate
Large bowl

Ingredients

4 veal chops (bone-in or boneless)
4 large eggs
½ tsp salt
¼ tsp freshly ground black pepper
1½ cups seasoned breadcrumbs (see page 116)
½ cup vegetable oil
Flaky sea salt, for garnish
Lemon wedges, for garnish

For the Salad

2 cups arugula
1 cup cherry tomatoes, halved
2 tbsp extra-virgin olive oil

1. Place the veal chops between two sheets of plastic wrap. Using a meat mallet, gently pound the chops to an even thickness of ½ inch (1.25cm).
2. Beat the eggs with the salt and pepper in a shallow bowl.
3. Add the seasoned breadcrumbs to a second shallow bowl.
4. Dip each veal chop into the egg mixture, ensuring it's fully coated. Then, press it into the breadcrumbs, covering all sides evenly.
5. Heat the vegetable oil in a large skillet over medium-high heat. Working in batches, fry the veal chops until golden brown and crispy, 2 or 3 minutes per side. Transfer the chops to a paper towel–lined plate to drain the excess oil.
6. Sprinkle each chop with flaky sea salt.
7. Toss the arugula and cherry tomatoes in a large bowl with the olive oil, and serve alongside the veal with lemon wedges on the side. Store leftovers in separate airtight containers in the refrigerator for up to 2 days. Reheat the veal in the oven at 375°F (190°C) on a large baking sheet for 10 to 12 minutes to maintain crispiness.

Osso Buco

(Braised Veal Shanks)

Equipment

Knife
Cutting board
Shallow bowl
Large Dutch oven or oven-safe braising pan with lid
Plate
Tongs
Wooden spoon

Ingredients

½ cup all-purpose flour
4–6 veal shanks, 1½ inches (3.75cm) thick, patted dry (about 3 lb/1.35kg total)
Kosher salt to taste
Freshly ground black pepper to taste
¼ cup extra-virgin olive oil, plus more as needed
1 medium yellow onion, finely diced
2 carrots, peeled and finely diced
2 celery stalks, finely diced
1 tsp tomato paste
1½ cups dry white wine
A few sprigs of fresh thyme
4 cups veal or beef stock

This is one of those dishes that takes time, but you're rewarded for every minute of it. Osso buco is all about depth of flavor—slow-cooked veal shanks, fragrant aromatics, and a rich broth that soaks into the meat until it's fall-off-the-bone tender. I've been making this dish for years, especially in the cooler months. It's perfect served alongside creamy risotto or polenta for Sunday dinner with the whole family around the table.

Prep Time:	Cook Time:	Total Time:	Serves:
20 minutes	3 hours	3 hours, 20 minutes	6

1. Preheat the oven to 350°F (180°C).
2. Add the flour to a shallow bowl.
3. Season both sides of the veal shanks generously with salt and pepper. Lightly dredge each piece in the flour, shaking off the excess.
4. Heat a large Dutch oven over medium-high heat, and add the olive oil. When the oil is hot, working in batches, brown the shanks until nicely golden, 2 or 3 minutes per side. Transfer to a plate, and set aside.
5. Carefully pour out and discard most of the oil in the pan, leaving behind about 2 tablespoons. Add the onion, carrots, and celery to the pan. Reduce the heat to medium, and sauté until the vegetables are soft and fragrant, 8 to 10 minutes.
6. Stir in the tomato paste, and cook for 1 or 2 minutes.
7. Pour in the white wine, and scrape up any browned bits from the bottom of the pan. Simmer the wine for 3 or 4 minutes. Season with a pinch of salt, pepper, and the thyme sprigs.
8. Return the veal shanks to the pan, arranging them so they fit snugly in a single layer. Pour in enough stock to cover them about ¾ of the way up. Bring the liquid to a gentle simmer.
9. Cover the Dutch oven with a lid, and transfer it to the oven. Cook for 2½ to 3 hours, or until the meat is tender and easily pulls away from the bone.
10. Serve the osso buco hot, spooning some of the pan sauce over the top. Store leftovers in an airtight container in the refrigerator for up to 3 days. Reheat gently in a medium frying pan over low heat for 10 to 12 minutes.

Sausage & Peppers

Sausage and peppers is one of those dishes that fills the whole kitchen with incredible aromas. This is how I've always made it—cooking the sausage so it's flavorful but not too greasy. The sweetness of the peppers and onions balances perfectly with the rich, pan-fried sausage. Serve it with some warm bread to make a sandwich or to soak up all that delicious olive oil.

Prep time:	Cook time:	Total time:	Serves:
10 minutes	25 minutes	35 minutes	4–6

Equipment

Knife
Cutting board
2 large skillets
Wooden spoon
Large pot
Colander
Paper towel

Ingredients

- 4 tbsp extra-virgin olive oil, divided
- 2 medium red bell peppers, ribs and seeds removed, and sliced
- 1 large white onion, sliced
- 1 tsp salt
- ½ tsp freshly ground black pepper
- 1 lb (450g) sweet Italian sausage

1. Heat 2 tablespoons olive oil in a large skillet over medium heat. Add the sliced bell peppers and onion, season with the salt and pepper, and sauté until soft and slightly caramelized, about 10 minutes.
2. Meanwhile, bring a large pot of water to a boil over high heat. Add the sausages, and boil for 3 or 4 minutes to reduce the excess fat. Drain the sausages, and pat them dry with a paper towel.
3. Heat the remaining 2 tablespoons olive oil in another large skillet over medium heat. Add the sausages, and pan-fry, turning occasionally, until golden brown and fully cooked, 8 to 10 minutes.
4. Add the peppers and onions to the sausage, and stir everything together. Cook for 5 to 6 minutes so the flavors meld.
5. Serve hot with warm Italian bread. Store leftovers in an airtight container in the refrigerator for up to 3 days. Reheat in a medium frying pan over low heat for 5 to 7 minutes or until warmed through.

Pork Chops Capricciosa

Crispy, golden, and topped with a bright, refreshing salad, pork chops capricciosa is a dish that's as delicious as it is satisfying. The combination of breaded pork, fresh greens, and tangy lemon makes every bite perfect. I love how the warm, crispy chop contrasts with the cool salad on top—it's a meal that always impresses.

Prep Time:	Cook Time:	Total Time:	Serves:
15 minutes	10 minutes	25 minutes	4

Equipment

Knife
Cutting board
Plastic wrap
Meat mallet
Whisk
2 shallow bowls
Large skillet
Tongs
Paper towels
Plate
Large mixing bowl

Ingredients

4 bone-in pork chops
4 large eggs
½ tsp salt
¼ tsp freshly ground black pepper
1½ cups seasoned breadcrumbs (see page 116)
½ cup vegetable oil
Flaky sea salt, for garnish
Lemon wedges, for garnish

For the Salad

2 cups mixed greens (such as arugula and radicchio)
½ small red onion, thinly sliced
½ cup cherry tomatoes, halved
2 tbsp extra-virgin olive oil
1 tbsp red wine vinegar
Salt and pepper to taste

1. Place the pork chops between two sheets of plastic wrap. Using a meat mallet, gently pound the chops to an even thickness of ½ inch (1.25cm). Set aside.
2. Beat the eggs with the salt and pepper in a shallow bowl.
3. Add the seasoned breadcrumbs to a second shallow bowl.
4. Dip each pork chop into the egg mixture, ensuring it's fully coated. Then press it into the breadcrumbs, covering all sides evenly.
5. Heat a large skillet over medium-high heat, and add the vegetable oil. Working in batches, fry the pork chops until golden brown and crispy, 3 to 4 minutes per side. Transfer to a paper towel–lined plate to drain the excess oil.
6. Sprinkle each chop with flaky sea salt, and let rest for a minute.
7. To make the salad, add the salad ingredients to a large mixing bowl, and toss well to combine.
8. Plate each pork chop and place equal amounts of the salad directly on top of each chop.
9. Serve immediately with lemon wedges on the side. Store leftovers in separate airtight containers in the refrigerator for up to 2 days. Reheat the chops in the oven at 375°F (190°C) for 10 to 12 minutes to maintain crispiness.

Stuffed Loin of Pork

This stuffed pork loin is one of my favorite dishes to make for our special Sunday dinners. The combination of savory sausage, tender broccoli rabe, and creamy provolone cheese inside a juicy pork loin makes for the perfect stand-out dish.

Prep Time:	Cook Time:	Total Time:	Serves:
20 minutes	1 hour, 10 minutes	1 hour, 30 minutes	6–8

Equipment

Knife
Cutting board
Large skillet
Wooden spoon
Kitchen twine
Roasting pan
Meat thermometer

Ingredients

4 tbsp extra-virgin olive oil, divided
2 small shallots, diced, divided
1 lb (450g) sweet Italian sausage, casings removed
1 bunch of broccoli rabe, chopped
1 tsp salt, plus more to taste
½ tsp freshly ground black pepper
¼ tsp crushed red pepper flakes
¼ cup grated Pecorino Romano
3–4 lb (1.35–2kg) boneless pork loin
6 slices provolone
3 garlic cloves, crushed
½ cup dry white wine

1. Preheat the oven to 375°F (190°C).
2. Heat 2 tablespoons olive oil in a large skillet over medium heat. Add ½ of the shallots, and cook until softened, about 3 minutes.
3. Add the sausage meat, breaking it up with a wooden spoon, and cook until fully browned, about 5 minutes.
4. Stir in the broccoli rabe, and season with the salt, pepper, and crushed red pepper flakes. Cook until the greens are tender, about 6 to 8 minutes.
5. Stir in the grated Pecorino Romano, and mix well. Remove from the heat, and set aside.
6. Make a vertical cut down the center of the pork loin and then carefully slice sideways into the original cut to create a larger pocket for the stuffing.
7. Tuck the slices of provolone into the pork loin pocket and then spread the sausage-and-broccoli-rabe mixture on top. Roll the pork loin tightly, and secure with kitchen twine.
8. Drizzle the remaining 2 tablespoons olive oil in a roasting pan, and scatter the rest of the shallots in the pan. Place the pork loin in the pan, season with salt and pepper, and add the crushed garlic over the top.
9. Bake for 20 minutes.
10. After 20 minutes, pour the white wine and ½ cup water into the pan, and cook for another 40 minutes, or until the pork reaches an internal temperature of 160°F (70°C).
11. Remove from the oven, and let the roast rest for 10 minutes.
12. Cut off the kitchen twine, slice the pork, and serve hot with a side of roasted potatoes. Store leftovers in an airtight container in the refrigerator for up to 3 days. Reheat in the oven at 350°F (180°C) for 15 to 20 minutes or until warmed through.

Rack of Lamb

Lamb chops are a special dish in my kitchen, perfect for a holiday or Sunday dinner with family. I like to keep things uncomplicated—good ingredients don't need much else. With a garlicky herb crust, a quick sear, and a slow roast, these lamb chops come out tender and packed with flavor every time.

Prep Time:	Cook Time:	Total Time:	Serves:
15 minutes	30 minutes	45 minutes	4

Equipment

Knife
Cutting board
Paper towel
Small mixing bowl
Large oven-safe skillet
Meat thermometer

Ingredients

1 rack of lamb (about 8 chops)
2 tbsp extra-virgin olive oil, divided
4 garlic cloves, minced
1 tbsp fresh rosemary, chopped
1 tbsp fresh thyme, chopped
1 tsp salt
½ tsp freshly ground black pepper
½ tsp crushed red pepper flakes (optional)

1. Preheat the oven to 400°F (200°C).
2. Pat the rack of lamb dry with a paper towel, and trim any excess fat.
3. Combine 1 tablespoon olive oil, the minced garlic, rosemary, thyme, salt, pepper, and red pepper flakes (if using) in a small mixing bowl. Rub this mixture all over the lamb.
4. Heat a large oven-safe skillet over medium-high heat, and add the remaining 1 tablespoon olive oil. Add the lamb, and sear until golden brown, about 2 minutes per side.
5. Transfer the skillet to the oven, and roast for about 15 minutes, or until the internal temperature of the lamb reaches 130°F (55°C) for medium-rare.
6. Remove from the oven and let the lamb rest for 10 minutes before slicing into chops.
7. Serve warm, preferably with roasted vegetables or a simple salad. Store leftovers in an airtight container in the refrigerator for up to 3 days. Reheat in the oven at 350°F (180°C) for 12 to 15 minutes or until warmed through.

Steak Pizzaiola

This dish is a perfect example of how a few simple ingredients can turn into something incredible. The rib-eye steaks soak up all the rich flavors of the tomato sauce, oregano, and garlic, making every bite tender and full of flavor. I always serve this dish with fresh bread to soak up every last drop of the sauce.

Prep Time:	Cook Time:	Total Time:	Serves:
10 minutes	30 minutes	40 minutes	4

Equipment

Knife
Cutting board
2 large skillets
Wooden spoon
Tongs

Ingredients

4 tbsp extra-virgin olive oil, divided
4 garlic cloves
4 plum tomatoes, crushed
1 tsp dried oregano
2 tbsp chopped fresh parsley
1 tsp salt, plus more to taste
½ tsp freshly ground black pepper
4 boneless rib-eye steaks
Flaky sea salt

1. Heat 2 tablespoons olive oil in a large skillet over medium heat. Add the garlic, and cook until browned, about 2 minutes.
2. Add the crushed plum tomatoes, oregano, parsley, salt, and pepper. Stir to combine, and simmer the sauce for 15 to 20 minutes.
3. Heat the remaining 2 tablespoons olive oil in a separate skillet over medium-high heat.
4. While the oil heats, season the rib-eye steaks generously with flaky sea salt.
5. Add the steaks to the skillet, and sear until browned but not fully cooked through, 2 or 3 minutes per side.
6. Transfer the steaks to the skillet with the tomato sauce, and cook in the sauce for another 5 minutes, flipping once halfway so they absorb all the flavors.
7. Serve the steaks hot with plenty of fresh Italian bread to soak up the sauce. Store leftovers in an airtight container in the refrigerator for up to 2 days. Reheat gently in a large frying pan over medium heat for 5 to 7 minutes.

Baccalà al Sugo

(Salted Cod in Tomato Sauce)

In my house, this was always just called baccalà (or salted cod), but when I think about it, baccalà al sugo (salted cod in sauce) is probably the more accurate name. It's a dish that brings everyone to the table—especially on those Sundays during the holidays. The salted cod, when rehydrated and fried, soaks up the flavor of the garlicky tomato sauce like nothing else. This recipe takes a little planning ahead, but it's worth every minute.

Prep Time:	Cook Time:	Total Time:	Serves:
30 minutes (plus 3 days soaking time)	40 minutes	1 hour, 10 minutes	6–8

Equipment

Knife
Cutting board
Large container
Paper towels
Shallow bowl
Large skillet
Plate
Large saucepan or deep skillet
Wooden spoon

Ingredients

- 3 lb (1.35kg) dried salt cod (baccalà), cut into roughly 4 × 3-inch (10 × 7.5cm) pieces
- All-purpose flour, for dredging
- Vegetable oil, for frying
- ¼ cup extra-virgin olive oil
- 3 garlic cloves, peeled and smashed
- 2 cups tomato purée (passata di pomodoro) or passata
- 1 dried hot red pepper, or to taste
- Pinch of kosher salt
- 2 tbsp chopped fresh parsley

1. Place the cod in a large container, and cover it completely with cold water. Let soak at room temperature for 3 days, changing the water once a day.
2. After 3 days, remove the cod from the water. Pat each piece dry with paper towels.
3. Place the flour in a shallow bowl. Dredge each piece of fish in the flour, shaking off any excess.
4. Heat a large skillet over medium-high heat, and add 2 inches (5cm) vegetable oil. When the oil is hot, and working in batches, add the cod and fry until golden on both sides, 4 to 6 minutes. Transfer to a paper towel–lined plate. Set aside.
5. Heat the olive oil in a large saucepan or a separate deep skillet over medium heat. When the oil is hot, add the garlic cloves and cook until golden brown, 1 to 2 minutes. Remove and discard the garlic.
6. Add the tomato purée, dried hot pepper, and the salt to the saucepan, and stir to combine. Reduce the heat to low, and simmer the sauce for about 15 minutes.
7. Gently nestle the fried baccalà in the sauce. Simmer, occasionally spooning the sauce over the cod, for 10 to 15 minutes.
8. Sprinkle with the fresh parsley, and serve hot, preferably with crusty bread to soak up the sauce. Store leftovers in an airtight container in the refrigerator for up to 2 days. Reheat gently in a pan over low heat for 5 to 7 minutes.

Cioppino

Cioppino isn't something I grew up with in Italy, but after coming to America, I learned how to make it. It's a true Italian American invention, and it reminds me how food always finds a way to bring people together, no matter where they come from. This dish is hearty, briny, and full of flavor. When I make it, I like to serve it with toasted bread, rubbed with a little garlic, and a nice glass of wine.

Prep time:	Cook time:	Total time:	Serves:
20 minutes	45 minutes	1 hour, 5 minutes	6

Equipment

Knife
Cutting board
Large pot with lid
Wooden spoon
Ladle

Ingredients

¼ cup extra-virgin olive oil
1 medium yellow onion, finely chopped
4 garlic cloves, minced
½ tsp crushed red pepper flakes, or to taste
¼ cup tomato paste
1½ cups dry white wine
28 oz (800g) can crushed San Marzano tomatoes
3 cups seafood stock, or 2 cups water with 1 cup clam juice
Kosher salt to taste
Freshly ground black pepper to taste
1 lb (450g) littleneck clams, scrubbed
1 lb (450g) mussels, scrubbed and debearded
1 lb (450g) shrimp, peeled and deveined
1 lb (450g) scallops
1 lb (450g) firm whitefish (like cod or halibut), cut into large chunks
Freshly chopped parsley, for garnish

1. Heat a large pot over medium heat, and add the olive oil. When the oil is hot, add the onion and cook until softened, 6 to 8 minutes.
2. Add the garlic and red pepper flakes, and cook until fragrant, 1 minute.
3. Stir in the tomato paste, and cook for 2 minutes.
4. Pour in the white wine, and scrape the bottom of the pot as you mix it in. Reduce the heat to low, and let the wine simmer until it reduces by about half, about 5 minutes.
5. Add the crushed tomatoes and seafood stock to the pot, and season with salt and pepper. Bring to a simmer, and cook, uncovered, for 15 to 20 minutes to allow the flavors to come together.
6. Add the clams and mussels, cover, and cook until they start to open, about 5 minutes.
7. Add the shrimp, scallops, and fish. Stir gently, and cook, uncovered, until everything is cooked through and the shellfish are fully opened, 5 to 7 minutes. Discard any shellfish that don't open.
8. Taste and adjust the seasonings to your liking. Ladle the stew into bowls, and top with fresh parsley.
9. Serve with toasted crusty bread on the side for dipping. Cioppino is best eaten the day it's made, but leftovers can be refrigerated for up to 2 days. Reheat gently in a medium frying pan over medium heat for 4 to 5 minutes. Be careful not to overcook the seafood.

Stuffed Calamari

Every time I make stuffed calamari, it reminds me of Christmas Eve, when we get together with all of our immediate and extended family as well as our friends. This recipe is a classic in my kitchen and something that always makes people stop and say "Wow." The trick is to not overstuff the calamari and to cook it just right so it's tender and full of flavor.

Prep time:	Cook time:	Total time:	Serves:
30 minutes	1 hour	1 hour, 30 minutes	6

Equipment

Knife
Cutting board
Large mixing bowl
Wooden spoon
Small spoon
Toothpicks or kitchen twine
Large sauté pan or Dutch oven with lid
Tongs
Plate

Ingredients

- 8 oz (225g) shrimp, peeled, deveined, and finely chopped
- 4 oz (115g) squid tentacles, finely chopped
- ½ cup plain breadcrumbs
- 2 tbsp finely chopped fresh parsley
- 4 tbsp extra-virgin olive oil, plus more as needed, divided
- 2 garlic cloves, minced
- Salt and freshly ground black pepper to taste
- 12 medium calamari tubes
- ½ medium yellow onion, finely diced
- 28 oz (800g) can crushed San Marzano tomatoes
- ¼ tsp crushed red pepper flakes (optional)
- Fresh basil, for garnish

1. Add the shrimp, squid tentacles, breadcrumbs, parsley, 2 tablespoons olive oil, and garlic in a large mixing bowl, and season with salt and pepper. Mix well until the filling just comes together. It should be moist but not wet.
2. Using a small spoon, carefully fill each calamari tube about ¾ full with the filling mixture. Don't overstuff or they might burst. Seal each with a toothpick or tie off with kitchen twine.
3. Heat the remaining 2 tablespoons olive oil in a large sauté pan over medium heat. Add the stuffed calamari, and sear until lightly golden, 2 minutes per side. Transfer the calamari to a plate, and set aside.
4. Add the onion to the sauté pan, with a little more oil if needed, and sauté until soft, about 5 minutes.
5. Add the crushed tomatoes and red pepper flakes (if using), season with salt and pepper, and simmer for 10 minutes.
6. Add the stuffed calamari to the sauce. Cover the pan with a lid, reduce the heat to low, and cook for about 40 minutes, turning the calamari occasionally to ensure they cook evenly.
7. Remove the toothpicks or twine, and slice each calamari into thick rounds. Spoon extra sauce over the calamari, and garnish with fresh basil.
8. Serve warm with crusty bread or over pasta. Store leftovers in an airtight container in the refrigerator for up to 2 days. Reheat gently in a medium frying pan over medium heat for 4 to 6 minutes, adding a bit of sauce to keep the calamari tender.

Eggplant Parmigiana

Equipment

Knife
Cutting board
Large pot
Wooden spoon
3 shallow bowls
Whisk
Large skillet
Tongs
Paper towels
Plate
Baking sheet

Ingredients

4 tbsp extra-virgin olive oil
3 garlic cloves
3 cups tomato purée (passata di pomodoro)
1½ tsp salt, divided
½ tsp freshly ground black pepper, divided
¼ cup fresh basil, plus more for garnish
1 cup all-purpose flour
3 large eggs, beaten
1½ cups seasoned breadcrumbs (see page 116)
2 large eggplants, skinned and sliced into pieces ½ inch (1.25cm) thick
Vegetable oil, for frying
1 cup grated Parmigiano-Reggiano, plus more for garnish
8 oz (225g) low-moisture mozzarella, sliced

Crispy fried eggplant layered with rich tomato sauce, melted mozzarella, and plenty of grated cheese, this eggplant parmigiana makes for a comforting and delicious meal. This is how I've been making it for years, just the way my family loves it.

Prep Time:	Cook Time:	Total Time:	Serves:
30 minutes	1 hour	1 hour, 30 minutes	6–8

1. Heat the olive oil in a large pot over medium heat. Add the whole garlic cloves, and cook until golden brown, about 2 minutes.
2. Pour in the tomato purée, and season with 1 teaspoon salt, ¼ teaspoon pepper, and the basil. Stir well and let the sauce simmer, stirring occasionally, for about 30 minutes.
3. Meanwhile, preheat the oven to 375°F (190°C).
4. Add the flour to one shallow bowl.
5. Beat the eggs with the remaining ½ teaspoon salt and ¼ teaspoon pepper in a second shallow bowl.
6. Add the seasoned breadcrumbs to a third shallow bowl.
7. Coat each eggplant slice in the flour, dip it in the egg mixture, and coat it with the breadcrumbs.
8. Add 2 inches (5cm) vegetable oil to a large skillet, and heat over medium heat. Working in batches, fry the eggplant slices until golden brown on both sides, about 2 minutes per side. Using tongs, transfer the eggplant to a paper towel–lined plate to drain the excess oil.
9. Dip each fried eggplant slice in the tomato sauce, and lay the slices on a baking sheet. Sprinkle generously with 1 cup Parmigiano-Reggiano, top with the mozzarella slices, and finish with more tomato sauce.
10. Bake for 20 to 25 minutes, until the cheese is melted and bubbling.
11. Remove from the oven and finish with more grated Parmigiano-Reggiano and fresh basil.
12. Serve hot. Store leftovers in an airtight container in the refrigerator for up to 3 days. Reheat in the oven at 350°F (180°C) for 12 to 15 minutes or until warmed through.

INSALATE
(Salads)

Panzanella Salad

Panzanella is a classic Italian bread salad that uses simple ingredients to create something delicious. This dish is a great way to use up stale bread, as it absorbs all the bright and fresh flavors of the tomatoes, basil, and olive oil. Although we always used to make it by necessity of using what we had around, we still prepare it today because it's just that delicious. It's a perfect salad that I love to serve at family gatherings.

Prep time:	Cook time:	Total time:	Serves:
15 minutes (plus 30 minutes resting time)	None	15 minutes	4–6

Equipment

Knife
Cutting board
Large salad bowl
Tongs

Ingredients

- 4 cups stale bread, cut into 1-inch (2.5cm) cubes
- 4 large ripe tomatoes, chopped
- ½ medium red onion, thinly sliced
- ¼ cup extra-virgin olive oil
- ½ tsp kosher salt
- ¼ tsp freshly ground black pepper
- ½ cup fresh basil leaves, torn

1. Add the bread, tomatoes, and red onion to a large salad bowl. Drizzle with the olive oil, and season with the salt and pepper.
2. Toss well to combine, and let the salad sit for about 30 minutes, stirring occasionally, so the bread can soak up the flavors.
3. Just before serving, add the basil and toss gently to combine.
4. Serve at room temperature. Panzanella is best enjoyed fresh, but leftovers can be stored in an airtight container in the refrigerator for up to 1 day.

Arugula Salad

This is one of those salads that proves simple really is best. I've been making this for years—just a handful of good ingredients, tossed together right before dinner—and it always disappears quickly. It's bright, fresh, and full of flavor, and it makes the perfect side for just about anything. For the best results, use the nicest olive oil you have for drizzling.

Prep Time:	Cook Time:	Total Time:	Serves:
10 minutes	3 minutes (optional)	10 minutes	4

Equipment

Knife
Cutting board
Small skillet (optional)
Large salad bowl
Tongs or salad servers

Ingredients

3 tbsp pine nuts
4 cups arugula
1 cup grape tomatoes, halved
Extra-virgin olive oil, for drizzling
Kosher salt to taste
Freshly ground black pepper to taste
1/3 cup shaved Parmigiano-Reggiano

1. If you'd like to toast the pine nuts, place them in a small, dry skillet over medium heat. Toast, stirring frequently until golden and fragrant, 2 or 3 minutes. Remove from the heat and let cool.
2. Add the arugula, grape tomatoes, and pine nuts to a large salad bowl. Drizzle with the extra-virgin olive oil and then season with the kosher salt and pepper.
3. Toss gently until everything is combined.
4. Top with the shaved Parmigiano-Reggiano, and serve immediately.
5. This salad is best enjoyed fresh. If you need to store it, store the salad and the dressing in separate airtight containers and combine just before serving to prevent the arugula from wilting.

Potato Salad

American fans of potato salad might be shocked to learn this version has no mayo in sight! This potato salad is light, bright, and full of the flavors I grew up with in Italy. The sweet cherry tomatoes, the fragrant basil, and a good drizzle of extra-virgin olive oil make all the difference. I've been making this salad for years, and every time I serve it, someone always asks for the recipe. Use the nicest olive oil you have for best results!

Prep Time:	Cook Time:	Total Time:	Serves:
15 minutes (plus cooling time)	20 minutes	35 minutes	6

Equipment

Knife
Cutting board
Large pot
Colander
Small knife (optional)
Large salad bowl
Tongs

Ingredients

2 lb (1kg) Yukon Gold potatoes
1 cup cherry tomatoes, halved
½ medium red onion, thinly sliced
½ cup diced celery hearts
⅓ cup fresh basil leaves, torn
¼ tsp garlic powder
½ tsp dried oregano
⅓ cup extra-virgin olive oil
Kosher salt to taste
Freshly ground black pepper to taste

1. Add the potatoes to a large pot, and cover with cold water. Set over high heat, bring to a boil, and then reduce the heat to low and simmer until fork-tender, 15 to 20 minutes. Drain the potatoes and let them cool enough to handle.
2. Using your hands or a small knife, peel the skins off the potatoes and then slice them into rounds ½ inch (1.25cm) thick. Allow them to finish cooling.
3. Add the cooled potatoes, cherry tomatoes, red onion, celery hearts, and basil to a large salad bowl. Sprinkle with the garlic powder and dried oregano, drizzle with the extra-virgin olive oil, and season with kosher salt and freshly ground pepper.
4. Toss gently until everything is combined.
5. Serve at room temperature or slightly chilled. Store leftovers in an airtight container in the refrigerator for up to 2 days. Let sit at room temperature for 10 to 15 minutes before serving.

Pesto Pasta Salad

This isn't your average pasta salad. My version is bright, flavorful, and full of love. The homemade pesto brings the whole dish together, and the combination of potatoes and green beans makes it hearty enough to serve as a full meal.

Prep Time:	Cook Time:	Total Time:	Serves:
25 minutes	25 minutes	50 minutes (plus cooling time)	6

Equipment

Knife
Cutting board
Food processor or blender
Large pot
Slotted spoon
Colander
Medium skillet
Large bowl
Tongs

Ingredients

For the Pesto

½ cup pine nuts
4 cups packed fresh basil leaves
2 garlic cloves
1 cup extra-virgin olive oil
½ cup grated Parmigiano-Reggiano
Kosher salt to taste
Freshly ground black pepper to taste

For the Salad

3 medium Yukon Gold potatoes, peeled and cut into 1-inch (2.5cm) cubes
8 oz (225g) green beans, trimmed and cut into 2-inch (5cm) pieces
2 tbsp extra-virgin olive oil, plus more for serving
2 garlic cloves, sliced
Kosher salt to taste
Freshly ground black pepper to taste
1 lb (450g) fusilli pasta
Grated Parmigiano-Reggiano, for serving

1. To make the pesto, add the pine nuts, basil, and garlic to a food processor or blender. Pulse a few times to break down everything. With the motor running, slowly stream in the olive oil until a smooth sauce forms. Stir in the Parmigiano-Reggiano, and season with salt and pepper. Set aside.
2. To make the salad, bring a large pot of salted water to a boil over high heat. Add the cubed potatoes and cook until just fork-tender, 8 to 10 minutes. Using a slotted spoon, transfer the cooked potatoes to a plate and set aside to cool.
3. Add the green beans to the same pot of boiling water, and boil until tender but still vibrant, 4 or 5 minutes. Drain and let cool. Reserve the pot of boiling water.
4. Heat the olive oil in a medium skillet over medium heat. When the oil is hot, add the sliced garlic and sauté until golden, 1 or 2 minutes.
5. Add the cooked green beans, season with salt and pepper, and sauté for 2 or 3 minutes. Remove from the heat, and set aside to cool.
6. In the same pot of boiling water, cook the pasta according to the package instructions until al dente. Drain and set aside to cool.
7. When everything has cooled to room temperature, combine the pasta, potatoes, and green beans in a large bowl. Add the pesto, and toss until well coated.
8. Finish with an extra drizzle of olive oil, more salt and pepper, and a sprinkle of grated Parmigiano-Reggiano.
9. Serve at room temperature. Store leftovers in an airtight container in the refrigerator for up to 2 days. Allow to come to room temperature before serving.

Beet Salad

I love this salad because it's as beautiful as it is delicious. The golden and red beets bring such vibrant colors to the dish, and the creamy goat cheese combined with the crunch of the pistachios makes every bite special. It's the kind of salad that feels fancy but couldn't be simpler to make.

Prep time:	Cook time:	Total time:	Serves:
15 minutes (plus cooling time)	45 minutes	1 hour	6

Equipment

Large pot
Colander
Paper towels or clean kitchen towel
Knife
Cutting board
Large mixing bowl
Tongs
Serving bowl

Ingredients

6 medium red and golden beets, rinsed under cold water

¼ cup extra-virgin olive oil, plus more for drizzling

Kosher salt to taste

Freshly ground black pepper to taste

4 oz (115g) goat cheese, crumbled

⅓ cup shelled pistachio nuts

1 Add the beets to a large pot, and cover with water. Set over high heat, bring to a boil, and then reduce the heat to low and simmer until the beets are fork-tender, 40 to 45 minutes. Drain the beets and let them cool enough to handle.

2 Using a paper towel or clean kitchen towel, gently rub off the beet skins. Slice the peeled beets into rounds ½ inch (1.25cm) thick, and allow them to finish cooling completely.

3 Add the sliced beets to a large mixing bowl. Drizzle with the olive oil, and season with salt and pepper.

4 Toss gently until everything is combined.

5 Add the crumbled goat cheese and pistachios, and mix gently until everything is evenly distributed.

6 Transfer the salad to a serving bowl, and serve at room temperature. Store leftovers in an airtight container in the refrigerator for up to 2 days. Allow the salad to come to room temperature before serving.

Classic Tricolor Salad

This refreshing salad is a staple on my table, especially when I want something light to balance a hearty meal. It's not just beautiful; it's crisp, peppery, and perfectly dressed with good olive oil and a touch of balsamic. The three colors of this salad—green arugula, white endive, and red radicchio—are the colors of the Italian flag!

Prep time:	Cook time:	Total time:	Serves:
10 minutes	none	10 minutes	4

Equipment

Knife
Cutting board
Large salad bowl
Tongs

Ingredients

2 Belgian endives, sliced
2 cups arugula
1 small head of radicchio, chopped
2 tbsp extra-virgin olive oil
1 tbsp balsamic vinegar
Kosher salt to taste
Freshly ground black pepper to taste

1. Add the sliced endives, arugula, and chopped radicchio to a large salad bowl. Drizzle with the olive oil and balsamic vinegar, and season with the salt and pepper.
2. Toss gently until everything is evenly coated.
3. Serve immediately at room temperature. This salad is best enjoyed fresh, but leftovers can be stored in an airtight container in the refrigerator for up to 1 day.

Endive Salad

This simple and colorful salad always reminds me of Sundays in the springtime. With bright, crunchy vegetables and fresh bocconcini, it's a refreshing addition to any meal. I used to make this when the weather first started to warm up and everyone wanted something light. The colors always felt happy to me—a little taste of the season right on the table. It's quick to put together, but it looks beautiful, and that's what makes it special.

Prep Time:	Cook Time:	Total Time:	Serves:
10 minutes	None	10 minutes	4

Equipment

Knife
Cutting board
Large salad bowl
Tongs

Ingredients

2 Belgian endives, sliced
1 small head of radicchio, chopped
1 cup cherry tomatoes, halved
1 cup bocconcini, drained
2 tbsp extra-virgin olive oil
Juice of 1 lemon
Kosher salt to taste
Freshly ground black pepper to taste

1. Add the endives, radicchio, cherry tomatoes, and bocconcini to a large salad bowl. Drizzle with the olive oil and lemon juice, and season with the salt and pepper.
2. Toss gently until everything is combined.
3. Serve immediately at room temperature. This salad is best enjoyed fresh, but leftovers can be stored in an airtight container in the refrigerator for up to 1 day.

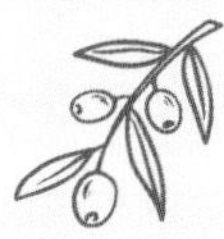

Fennel Salad

I love making this salad when fennel is in season. The sweet citrus from the blood orange pairs perfectly with the incredible Sicilian olives and the crunch of the fennel. This salad is fresh, vibrant, and unmistakably Mediterranean. I remember my mother slicing fennel with her favorite knife, allowing me to sample it as she prepared the salad. It's the kind of dish that feels like sunshine on the table—bright, balanced, and simple, the way good food should be. A drizzle of Nonna's Olive Oil brings it all together and reminds me of home in every bite.

Prep Time:	Cook Time:	Total Time:	Serves:
15 minutes	None	15 minutes	4

Equipment

Knife
Cutting board
Large salad bowl
Tongs

Ingredients

2 fennel bulbs, stems and ends removed, halved, and thinly sliced
½ blood orange, peeled and diced
⅓ cup black Sicilian olives
2 tbsp extra-virgin olive oil
Kosher salt to taste
Freshly ground black pepper to taste

1. Add the sliced fennel, blood orange, and black Sicilian olives to a large salad bowl. Drizzle with the olive oil, and season with the salt and pepper.
2. Toss gently until everything is well combined.
3. Serve at room temperature. Store leftovers in an airtight container in the refrigerator for up to 1 day. Allow the salad to come to room temperature before serving.

CONTORNI

(Side Dishes)

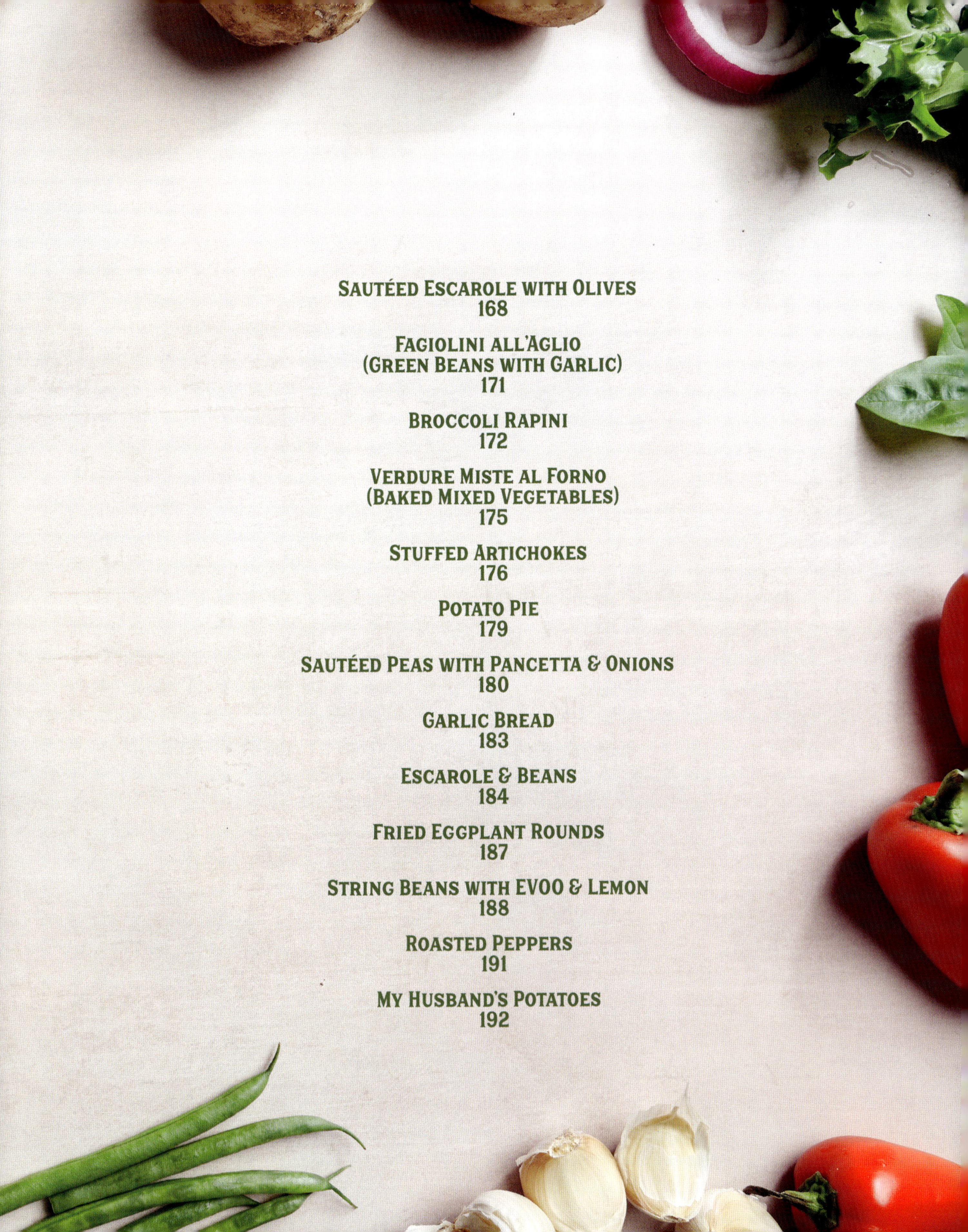

Sautéed Escarole *with Olives*

Although it's not so common in America, escarole was always on the table when I was growing up in southern Italy. We prepared it many different ways, and this is one of my favorites. The combination of garlic, anchovies, and black olives gives this dish a deep, savory flavor with just the right amount of heat. It's simple and quick, the perfect side dish to any meal.

Prep time:	Cook time:	Total time:	Serves:
10 minutes	15 minutes	25 minutes	4

Equipment

Colander
Knife
Cutting board
Large skillet
Wooden spoon

Ingredients

3 tbsp extra-virgin olive oil
3 garlic cloves
4 anchovy fillets
½ cup black olives, pitted
1 large head escarole, washed and chopped into large pieces
1 tsp kosher salt
¼ tsp crushed red pepper flakes

1. Heat the olive oil in a large skillet over medium heat. Add the garlic, and cook until golden brown, about 2 minutes.
2. Add the anchovy fillets, breaking them up with a wooden spoon as they dissolve into the oil. Stir in the black olives.
3. Add the escarole, and season with the salt and crushed red pepper flakes. Stir to combine.
4. Cook, stirring occasionally, until the escarole is tender and wilted, 5 to 10 minutes.
5. Serve warm as a side dish or with fresh bread. Store leftovers in an airtight container in the refrigerator for up to 2 days. Reheat gently in a medium frying pan over medium heat for 3 to 5 minutes, adding a drizzle of olive oil.

FAGIOLINI ALL'AGLIO

(Green Beans with Garlic)

When I was growing up, dishes didn't need to be fancy to be good—they just needed to be made right. Fagiolini all'Aglio is one of those simple, honest recipes that always found its way onto our dinner table. Just green beans, garlic, and olive oil. That's it. But when made with love—and the right technique—this dish becomes something you can't stop picking at. I serve this warm or at room temperature, often alongside an array of Sunday dinner classics.

PREP TIME:	COOK TIME:	TOTAL TIME:	SERVES:
10 MINUTES	20 MINUTES	30 MINUTES	4–6

EQUIPMENT

Knife
Cutting board
Large pot
Colander
Large skillet
Wooden spoon

INGREDIENTS

- 1½ pounds green beans (fagiolini), ends trimmed
- 3 tbsp extra-virgin olive oil
- 4 garlic cloves, peeled and smashed
- ½ tsp kosher salt
- ¼ tsp freshly ground black pepper
- Pinch of crushed red pepper flakes (optional)

1. Bring a large pot of generously salted water to a boil over high heat. Add the green beans, and cook until just tender but still bright green, 5 to 7 minutes. Drain and set aside.
2. Heat a large skillet over medium heat, and add the olive oil. When the oil is hot, add the garlic and cook until golden brown, 2 or 3 minutes. Keep an eye on it—you want the garlic golden, not burned.
3. Add the green beans to the skillet. Season with the salt, pepper, and crushed red pepper flakes (if using). Sauté, stirring occasionally, until the green beans have soaked up all that garlicky flavor and are slightly blistered, 5 to 7 minutes.
4. Remove from the heat and serve warm or at room temperature. This dish is best enjoyed the same day, but leftovers can be stored in an airtight container in the refrigerator for up to 3 days. Reheat with an extra drizzle of olive oil in a medium frying pan over medium heat for about 3 minutes.

Broccoli Rapini

Equipment

Knife
Cutting board
Large pot
Colander
Large pan
Wooden spoon

Ingredients

6½ tsp salt, divided
1 lb (450g) broccoli rapini, trimmed
2 tbsp extra-virgin olive oil
4 garlic cloves, thinly sliced
¼ tsp red pepper flakes (optional)
¼ tsp freshly ground black pepper

I've been cooking broccoli rapini this way for as long as I can remember. It was always on the table when I was growing up, served alongside traditional entrées or just with a piece of good bread to soak up the olive oil. The secret is to blanch the broccoli rapini first to remove some of the bitterness and then sauté it with plenty of garlic and extra-virgin olive oil until it's tender and full of flavor. Simple and delicious, exactly the way it should be.

Prep Time:	Cook Time:	Total Time:	Serves:
5 minutes	10 minutes	15 minutes	4

1. Bring a large pot of water and 6 teaspoons salt to a boil over high heat. Add the broccoli rapini and blanch until tender, 2 to 3 minutes. Drain the broccoli rapini, and set aside.
2. Heat the olive oil in a large pan over medium heat. Add the sliced garlic and red pepper flakes (if using), and sauté until fragrant, about 1 minute.
3. Add the drained rapini to the pan and toss to coat in the garlic-infused oil. Season with the remaining ½ teaspoon salt and the pepper. Cook, stirring occasionally, until tender and well combined, 3 to 4 minutes.
4. Transfer to a serving dish and serve immediately. Store leftovers in an airtight container in the refrigerator for up to 3 days. Reheat in a skillet over medium heat for about 4 minutes.

Verdure Miste al Forno

(Baked Mixed Vegetables)

Equipment

Knife
Cutting board
Large baking sheet
Parchment paper (optional)
Large mixing bowl
Wooden spoon

Ingredients

- 2 medium zucchini, cut into thick slices
- 1 large red bell pepper, ribs and seeds removed, and cut into strips
- 1 large yellow bell pepper, ribs and seeds removed, and cut into strips
- 1 small eggplant, cubed
- 1 medium red onion, sliced
- 2 medium Yukon Gold potatoes, cubed
- 3 tbsp extra-virgin olive oil
- 3 garlic cloves, minced
- 1 tsp salt
- ½ tsp freshly ground black pepper
- ½ tsp dried oregano
- ½ tsp dried basil
- ½ tsp red pepper flakes (optional)
- Chopped fresh parsley, for garnish
- ¼ cup grated Pecorino Romano (optional)

Few things are better than a tray of beautifully roasted vegetables straight from the oven. This dish is smooth, flavorful, and the perfect way to use up whatever fresh produce you have on hand. The key is roasting everything just right—golden brown on the edges, tender on the inside, and kissed with extra-virgin olive oil and herbs. Serve it as a side, or enjoy it on its own with some warm bread.

Prep Time:	Cook Time:	Total Time:	Serves:
10 minutes	35 minutes	45 minutes	4–6

1. Preheat the oven to 400°F (200°C). Line a large baking sheet with parchment paper or lightly grease with olive oil.
2. Combine the zucchini, bell peppers, eggplant, onion, and potatoes in a large mixing bowl. Drizzle with the olive oil, and add the minced garlic, salt, pepper, oregano, basil, and red pepper flakes (if using). Toss everything together until well coated.
3. Spread the vegetables in a single layer on the prepared baking sheet to ensure even roasting.
4. Roast for 30 to 35 minutes, stirring halfway through, until the vegetables are tender and slightly caramelized at the edges.
5. Sprinkle the roasted vegetables with the fresh parsley and the grated Pecorino Romano (if using) before serving. Store leftovers in an airtight container in the refrigerator for up to 3 days. Reheat in the oven at 350°F (180°C) for 7 to 9 minutes for the best texture.

Stuffed Artichokes

Stuffed artichokes is a classic dish in my kitchen. The tender leaves soak up all the flavor from the garlicky, cheesy breadcrumb stuffing, and the slow simmering makes them perfectly tender. This dish is a labor of love, but it's always worth it when you pull apart the leaves and enjoy every bite.

Prep Time:	Cook Time:	Total Time:	Serves:
30 Minutes	55 Minutes	1 Hour, 25 Minutes	4

Equipment

Knife
Cutting board
2 large mixing bowls
Kitchen towel
Wooden spoon
Large skillet with lid

Ingredients

4 large artichokes
1 lemon, cut into wedges
4 garlic cloves, chopped and divided
¼ cup chopped fresh parsley
1 cup plain breadcrumbs
½ cup grated Parmigiano-Reggiano
1 tsp kosher salt
½ tsp freshly ground black pepper
4 tbsp extra-virgin olive oil, divided

1. Clean the artichokes by cutting off the stems and trimming the tops. Reserve the stems. Bang the artichokes lightly on the countertop to help open them up. Add the artichokes and lemon wedges to a large mixing bowl full of water, and let them soak for 20 minutes. Transfer the soaked artichokes to a clean kitchen towel to dry.
2. Combine 2 cloves of chopped garlic along with the parsley, breadcrumbs, Parmigiano-Reggiano, salt, and pepper in a second large mixing bowl.
3. Chop the reserved artichoke stems, and mix them into the filling.
4. Stuff the filling into the opened leaves of each artichoke, pressing it in gently. Set aside the stuffed artichokes.
5. Heat 2 tablespoons olive oil in a large skillet over medium heat. Add the remaining 2 cloves of chopped garlic, and cook until golden brown, about 2 minutes.
6. Add the stuffed artichokes to the pan, and sauté until the outsides are lightly browned, about 2 to 3 minutes.
7. Add ½ cup water to the pan, and cover the pan. Reduce the heat to low, and cook, adding small amounts of water as needed, until the artichokes are tender, 45 to 50 minutes.
8. Drizzle with the remaining 2 tablespoons olive oil before serving. Store leftovers in an airtight container in the refrigerator for up to 2 days. To reheat, preheat a large frying pan over medium heat then reduce the heat to low. Add the artichokes to the pan and heat for 12 to 14 minutes, adding a splash of water.

Potato Pie

This potato pie is one of my favorite comfort foods—creamy mashed potatoes, plenty of cheese, and a crispy breadcrumb topping. It's a dish that's easy to make but always feels special when it comes out of the oven, golden and bubbling.

Prep time:	Cook time:	Total time:	Serves:
20 minutes	1 hour, 15 minutes	1 hour, 35 minutes	6–8

Equipment

Knife
Cutting board
Large pot
Colander
Large mixing bowl
Potato masher
Wooden spoon
13 × 9 × 2-inch (33 × 23 × 5cm) baking dish

Ingredients

- 8 large Yukon Gold potatoes
- ¼ cup unsalted butter, plus 4 tbsp for topping
- 3 tbsp grated Pecorino Romano
- ½ tsp freshly ground black pepper
- 3 large eggs
- 1 cup seasoned breadcrumbs, divided
- 8 oz (225g) low-moisture mozzarella, sliced

1. Preheat the oven to 365°F (185°C).
2. Bring a large pot of water to a boil over high heat. Add the potatoes, and cook until fork-tender, about 20 minutes. Drain the potatoes and transfer to a large mixing bowl.
3. Mash the potatoes using a potato masher.
4. Stir in the ¼ cup butter until melted and fully incorporated.
5. Add the grated Pecorino Romano, pepper, and eggs. Mix well until fully combined.
6. Grease the baking dish with cooking spray, and coat the bottom and sides with half of the breadcrumbs.
7. Spread half of the mashed potato mixture into the baking dish, and smooth it to an even layer. Top with the sliced mozzarella and then cover with the remaining mashed potatoes, spreading them evenly to the edges and then sprinkle with the remaining breadcrumbs. Cut the remaining 4 tablespoons of butter into small pieces, and dot the top with the pieces.
8. Bake for 40 to 45 minutes or until golden brown and bubbling.
9. Let cool slightly before slicing and serving. Store leftovers in an airtight container in the refrigerator for up to 3 days. Reheat in the oven at 350°F (180°C) for 12 to 14 minutes, or until warmed through.

Sautéed Peas
with Pancetta and Onions

Equipment

Knife
Cutting board
Large skillet
Wooden spoon

Ingredients

2 tbsp extra-virgin olive oil
4 oz (115g) pancetta, diced
1 small yellow onion, finely chopped
12 oz (340g) frozen peas
1 tsp kosher salt, or to taste
½ tsp freshly ground black pepper, or to taste

This quick and flavorful side dish combines sweet peas with savory pancetta and onions, all brought together with the richness of extra-virgin olive oil (particularly if you use Nonna's Olive Oil). It's a simple, delicious addition to any Sunday dinner.

Prep Time:	Cook Time:	Total Time:	Serves:
5 minutes	15 minutes	20 minutes	4

1 Heat the olive oil in a large skillet over medium heat. Add the diced pancetta, and cook until it starts to crisp, 3 to 4 minutes.

2 Stir in the chopped onion, and sauté until softened, about 5 minutes.

3 Add the frozen peas, stir to combine, and cook until the peas are tender, 5 to 7 minutes.

4 Season with the salt and pepper, and stir well.

5 Serve warm. Store leftovers in an airtight container in the refrigerator for up to 2 days. Reheat gently in a small frying pan over medium heat for 4 to 5 minutes.

Garlic Bread

A side of warm, buttery garlic bread is a great accompaniment to any Italian meal. Crisp on the outside, soft on the inside, and packed with a rich garlic flavor, this simple yet delicious side dish is perfect for soaking up extra sauce or enjoying on its own. A touch of fresh parsley and a sprinkle of Pecorino Romano make it extra special.

PREP TIME:	COOK TIME:	TOTAL TIME:	SERVES:
5 MINUTES	10 MINUTES	15 MINUTES	4–6

Equipment

Knife
Cutting board
Serrated knife
Baking sheet
Small bowl
Wooden spoon
Pastry brush

Ingredients

- 1 loaf Italian bread, sliced in half lengthwise
- 4 tbsp unsalted butter, softened
- 2 tbsp extra-virgin olive oil
- 4 garlic cloves, minced
- ½ tsp salt
- ¼ tsp freshly ground black pepper
- 1 tbsp finely chopped fresh parsley
- 2 tbsp grated Pecorino Romano (optional)

1. Preheat the oven to 375°F (190°C).
2. Place the bread halves cut side up on a baking sheet.
3. Mix the butter, olive oil, garlic, salt, pepper, and parsley in a small bowl until well combined.
4. Evenly spread the garlic-butter mixture over the cut sides of the bread and sprinkle with Pecorino Romano (if using).
5. Bake for 8 to 10 minutes, until the bread is golden and crisp around the edges.
6. Slice into portions and serve warm. Store leftovers in an airtight container in the refrigerator for up to 2 days. Reheat in the oven at 375°F (190°C) for 6 to 7 minutes to restore crispiness.

Escarole & Beans

I grew up eating dishes like this all the time. In my house, simple meals like escarole and beans were a staple—not just because they were inexpensive to make, but also because they were hearty, delicious, and nourishing. This is true southern Italian cooking and what some might call "peasant food"—dishes made with a few humble ingredients that come together to create something healthy, comforting, and full of flavor. Maybe dishes like this are why Italians are known to live so long!

Prep Time:	Cook Time:	Total Time:	Serves:
10 minutes	30 minutes	40 minutes	4–6

Equipment

Knife
Cutting board
2 large pots
Colander
Wooden spoon

Ingredients

1 large head escarole, chopped and washed
¼ cup extra-virgin olive oil
6 garlic cloves
1 dried hot red pepper
1½ tsp kosher salt
½ tsp freshly ground black pepper
2 cups dried cannellini beans, boiled until tender and strained
Toasted bread, for serving

1. Bring a large pot of generously salted water to a boil over high heat. Add the escarole, and cook for about 10 minutes. Drain and set aside.
2. Heat the olive oil in a separate large pot over medium heat. Add the whole garlic cloves, and cook until golden brown, about 2 minutes.
3. Add the dried hot red pepper, and let it infuse for a moment.
4. Stir in the boiled escarole, and season with the salt and pepper.
5. Add the cooked cannellini beans, and stir to combine. Cook for 10 minutes to allow the flavors to meld.
6. Serve hot in bowls with a side of toasted bread. Store leftovers in an airtight container in the refrigerator for up to 2 days. Reheat gently in a medium frying pan over medium heat for about 4 minutes, adding a splash of water if needed.

Fried Eggplant Rounds

There's something so comforting about the smell of eggplant sizzling in olive oil. This is a dish I used to make often when I had extra eggplants. It's simple, crisp, and absolutely delicious. I like to enjoy these plain, but you can finish them with black pepper or a touch of grated Pecorino Romano if you'd like.

Prep time:	Cook time:	Total time:	Serves:
15 minutes (plus 30 minutes resting time)	20 minutes	35 minutes	4–6

Equipment

Knife
Cutting board
Paper towels
Baking sheet
Large skillet
Shallow bowl
Slotted spoon or tongs

Ingredients

- 2 medium eggplants, sliced into ¼-inch (6mm) rounds (about 1½ lb/680g total)
- Kosher salt
- Vegetable oil, for frying
- 1 cup all-purpose flour, for dredging
- Freshly ground black pepper (optional)

1. Lay the eggplant slices on a paper towel–lined baking sheet, and sprinkle both sides with salt. Let the eggplant sit for 20 to 30 minutes to draw out excess moisture and bitterness. Pat dry with more paper towels.
2. Heat a large skillet over medium heat, and add about ½ inch (1.25cm) vegetable oil.
3. Add the flour to a shallow bowl. While the oil is heating, dredge each slice of eggplant in the flour, shaking off any excess.
4. When the oil is hot, and working in batches, fry the eggplant slices until golden brown all over, 2 to 3 minutes per side. Be careful not to overcrowd the pan. Using a slotted spoon or tongs, transfer the fried eggplant rounds to a paper towel–lined plate or baking sheet to drain.
5. Finish with a sprinkle of salt and pepper (if using). Serve hot, warm, or at room temperature. These are best eaten fresh, but leftovers can be stored in an airtight container in the refrigerator for up to 2 days. Reheat in a medium skillet over medium heat for about 4 minutes, or in the oven at 375°F (190°C) for 10 minutes to keep them crispy.

STRING BEANS
with EVOO & Lemon

When I was growing up, this was one of the simplest side dishes we made. We didn't have it often, but we always had string beans in the garden, olive oil in the pantry, and lemons on the table. That's all you really need. This dish is still one of my favorites and makes its way to the dinner table frequently because it's light, refreshing, and comes together in no time.

PREP TIME:	COOK TIME:	TOTAL TIME:	SERVES:
10 MINUTES	8 MINUTES	18 MINUTES	4

EQUIPMENT

Knife
Cutting board
Large pot
Colander
Large bowl
Tongs or serving spoon
Microplane or zester (optional)

INGREDIENTS

1 lb (450g) string beans, ends trimmed
¼ cup extra-virgin olive oil
Juice of 1 lemon
½ tsp kosher salt, or to taste
¼ tsp freshly ground black pepper
Zest of 1 lemon (optional)

1. Bring a large pot of salted water to a boil over high heat. Add the string beans, and cook until tender but still bright green, 6 to 8 minutes. Drain the beans, and transfer them to a large bowl.
2. While the string beans are still warm, drizzle them with the olive oil and lemon juice and then season with the salt and pepper. Toss well to coat, and taste and adjust seasoning as needed.
3. Top with the lemon zest (if using) right before serving. Store leftovers in an airtight container in the refrigerator for up to 2 days. Bring to room temperature before serving, or enjoy chilled.

Roasted Peppers

When I was growing up, we always had roasted peppers in the house. We ate them as an antipasto, as a side dish, or just on a piece of bread. But let me tell you something funny: I roast them right on the stove burner, over the open flame! It can make a bit of a mess, but that's how I've always done it. The smell brings me right back to my mother's kitchen in Sarno.

Prep time:	Cook time:	Total time:	Serves:
10 minutes	15 minutes (plus 10 minutes steaming time and 15 minutes resting time)	25 minutes	4

Equipment

Kitchen torch or barbecue grill (optional)
Knife
Cutting board
Tongs
Large bowl
Plastic wrap or plate
Small serving platter

Ingredients

4 large red bell peppers
2 garlic cloves, thinly sliced
Pinch of salt
3 tbsp extra-virgin olive oil
Chopped fresh parsley (optional)

1. Place the bell peppers directly on your stove burners over a medium flame. Roast the peppers, turning them with tongs every few minutes, until the skin is completely charred and blackened on all sides, 2½ or 3 minutes per side. (Alternatively, if you don't have a gas stove, you can use a kitchen torch or barbecue grill to roast the peppers.)
2. Transfer the roasted peppers to a large bowl, cover with plastic wrap or a plate, and steam the peppers for about 10 minutes to make them easier to peel.
3. Using your hands, peel the charred skin from the roasted and steamed peppers. (Don't rinse them under water—you'll wash away the flavor!) Remove the stems, ribs, and seeds.
4. Slice the peppers into thin strips, and transfer them to a small serving platter. Add the sliced garlic and a generous pinch of salt, and drizzle with the extra-virgin olive oil. Toss gently to coat.
5. Let the peppers sit at room temperature for at least 15 minutes before serving and then garnish with the chopped parsley (if using). Store leftovers in an airtight container in the refrigerator for up to 4 days. Bring the leftover peppers to room temperature before serving. (They are even better the next day!)

My Husband's Potatoes

Equipment

Knife
Cutting board
7-inch (18cm) round baking dish
Wooden spoon

Ingredients

- 5 Yukon Gold potatoes, each cut into 3 or 4 pieces
- 3 tbsp extra-virgin olive oil
- 1 medium yellow onion, sliced
- 4 tbsp unsalted butter
- 1½ tsp kosher salt
- ½ tsp freshly ground black pepper

Most of the dishes I cook regularly are from generations-old family recipes, yet I learned this one from my American husband. While John was working as a waiter, he learned how to make a few dishes. This was one of them, and it has been a favorite in our home for years. The potatoes bake until they're golden and crispy on the outside while staying tender and buttery on the inside, and the combination of olive oil, butter, and onions gives them a rich, comforting flavor. As you can imagine, this is more than an incredible side dish to me. With every bite, I'm transported back to the days of my youth, sitting at the dinner table with my two little daughters and the love of my life.

Prep time:	Cook time:	Total time:	Serves:
10 minutes	50 minutes	60 minutes	4–6

1. Preheat the oven to 375°F (190°C).
2. Place the potato pieces in the baking dish. Pour 1 cup water and the extra-virgin olive oil over the potatoes. Scatter the sliced onion on top, and dot with pieces of the butter. Season with the salt and pepper and toss, ensuring everything is evenly coated.
3. Bake for 45 to 50 minutes, stirring occasionally, until the potatoes are crispy on the outside and soft on the inside.
4. Serve warm as a side dish. Store leftovers in an airtight container in the refrigerator for up to 3 days. Reheat in the oven at 350°F (180°C) for 12 to 14 minutes or until warmed through.

Dolci

(Desserts)

Pane degli Angeli

(Italian Angel Food Cake)

Equipment

- Microplane or zester
- 10-inch (25.5cm) springform pan or angel-food cake pan
- Parchment paper
- Sifter or fine-mesh sieve
- 2 large mixing bowls
- Mixer
- Rubber spatula
- Whisk
- Small bowl
- Toothpick
- Wire rack

Ingredients

- 1¼ cups all-purpose flour
- ¼ cup cornstarch
- 1 tbsp pane degli angeli baking powder, or 1 tbsp baking powder and a few drops of vanilla extract
- ½ tsp kosher salt
- 5 large eggs, at room temperature
- 1 cup granulated sugar
- Zest of 1 lemon
- 1 tsp vanilla extract
- ¼ cup whole milk
- ¼ cup vegetable oil or light olive oil
- Confectioners' sugar, for dusting

Pane degli angeli, or "bread of angels," is a light, airy Italian cake often associated with celebrations and holidays. In our family, it's the kind of cake you serve when you want something a little magical. With a delicate crumb and a heavenly scent of vanilla and citrus, it makes you close your eyes when you take a bite. Serve it with a dusting of confectioners' sugar, a dollop of whipped cream, or just as it is. Sometimes, the simplest cakes make the biggest impression.

Prep Time:	Cook Time:	Total Time:	Serves:
20 minutes	35 minutes	55 minutes	10–12

1. Preheat the oven to 350°F (180°C). Grease a 10-inch (25.5cm) springform pan or angel-food cake pan. If using a springform pan, line the bottom with parchment paper.
2. Sift together the flour, cornstarch, baking powder, and salt in a large mixing bowl. Set aside.
3. Add the eggs and granulated sugar to another large mixing bowl or the bowl of a stand mixer, and beat with a mixer on high until the mixture is pale, fluffy, and has tripled in volume, 5 to 7 minutes.
4. With a spatula, gently fold in the lemon zest and vanilla extract.
5. Whisk together the milk and oil in a small bowl or measuring cup. While gently folding with the spatula, slowly drizzle the milk mixture into the egg mixture.
6. Add the dry ingredients in three parts, folding gently after each addition until fully combined. Be careful not to overmix, which can deflate the batter.
7. Pour the batter into the prepared pan, and smooth the top.
8. Bake for 30 to 35 minutes, until the top is golden and a toothpick inserted into the center of the cake comes out clean.
9. Let cool in the pan for 10 minutes before transferring to a wire rack to cool completely.
10. Once cool, dust generously with confectioners' sugar before serving. Store covered at room temperature for up to 3 days. If desired, wrap individual slices in plastic wrap and freeze for up to 1 month. Thaw before serving.

Ciambellone

(Italian Ring Cake)

Equipment

10-inch (25.5cm) Bundt or tube pan
Sifter or fine-mesh sieve
Medium mixing bowl
Mixer
Microplane or zester
Large mixing bowl
Silicone spatula
Whisk
Toothpick
Wire rack

Ingredients

2½ cups all-purpose flour, sifted, plus more for dusting
½ cup salted butter, at room temperature
1 cup granulated sugar
4 large eggs, at room temperature
1 cup whole milk, at room temperature
2 tsp vanilla extract
1 tbsp baking powder
Zest of 2 lemons
Confectioners' sugar, for dusting

Ciambellone has always been the cake I turn to when I want a comforting dessert. It's perfect for breakfast with a cup of coffee, as a gentle afternoon treat, and of course, as a sweet ending for Sunday dinner. It's buttery, tender, and ever-so-lightly scented with lemon. Ciambellone is elegance in every bite.

Prep Time:	Cook Time:	Total Time:	Serves:
15 minutes	40 minutes	55 minutes	10–12

1 Preheat the oven to 350°F (180°C). Grease a Bundt pan thoroughly, and dust it with flour.

2 Add the butter and 1 cup granulated sugar to a medium mixing bowl, and cream with a mixer until light and fluffy, about 3 minutes.

3 Add the eggs one at a time, beating well after each. Mix in the milk and vanilla extract until well combined.

4 Whisk together the flour, baking powder, and lemon zest in a large mixing bowl or the bowl of a stand mixer.

5 Blending with a mixer on low, gradually add the dry mixture to the wet and beat until smooth, about 2 to 3 minutes.

6 Pour the batter into the prepared pan and smooth the top with a silicone spatula.

7 Bake for 35 to 40 minutes, until a toothpick inserted into the center of the cake comes out clean.

8 Let cool in the pan for 10 minutes before inverting onto a wire rack to cool completely.

9 Dust with the confectioners' sugar before serving. Store leftovers at room temperature, wrapped in foil or in an airtight container for up to 3 days. This cake also freezes well for up to 1 month. Thaw before serving.

Biscotti

Biscotti are a staple in every Italian or Italian American household. We've been making them with this exact same recipe for more than a century. These biscotti are a family tradition—crispy, golden, and perfect for dipping in coffee. The dough comes together easily, is tossed in the oven, sliced, and baked again for that signature biscotti crunch.

Prep Time:	Cook Time:	Total Time:	Yield:
15 minutes (plus 30 minutes chilling time)	40 minutes	55 minutes	36 biscotti

Equipment

2 baking sheets
Large mixing bowl
Mixer
Knife
Cutting board

Ingredients

3½ cups all-purpose flour
1 tsp baking powder
1 cup sugar
4 large eggs

1 Lightly grease 2 baking sheets.

2 Add the flour, baking powder, sugar, and eggs to a large mixing bowl or the bowl of a stand mixer. Blend with a mixer on medium speed until a smooth dough forms, 3 to 4 minutes.

3 Divide the dough into 2 equal-size pieces. Place the pieces on the prepared baking sheets, evenly spaced so they don't touch. Refrigerate for 30 minutes.

4 Preheat the oven to 375°F (190°C).

5 Bake the dough pieces for 20 to 25 minutes, or until golden brown.

6 Remove from the oven and carefully slice each piece into biscotti shapes.

7 Place the sliced biscotti back on the baking sheets, return to the oven, and bake for 10 to 15 minutes, until they are crisp and crunchy.

8 Allow to cool completely before serving. Store in an airtight container at room temperature for up to 2 weeks.

TIRAMISU

EQUIPMENT

Espresso machine or stovetop moka pot
Small bowl
2 large mixing bowls
Mixer
13 × 9 × 2-inch (33 × 23 × 5cm) baking dish
Rubber spatula
Sifter

INGREDIENTS

2 cups freshly brewed espresso
6 tbsp granulated sugar, divided
5 tbsp Kahlúa, divided
2 eggs
1 egg yolk
16 oz (450g) mascarpone cheese
1 cup heavy cream
2 tbsp confectioners' sugar
1 package ladyfinger cookies (about 48 cookies)
Dark chocolate cocoa powder, for dusting

Tiramisu has been a beloved Italian dessert for generations, and its name, meaning "pick-me-up" in Italian, perfectly describes the boost of energy you get from its rich espresso and delicate layers of mascarpone. Although its exact origins are debated, many believe tiramisu first appeared in northern Italy, which would make sense, considering this isn't something I learned how to make when I was living in the south. I've been making this for years, however, and it's always a hit at the table. The layers of espresso-soaked ladyfingers, creamy mascarpone, and dusting of cocoa make for the ultimate indulgence.

PREP TIME:	COOK TIME:	TOTAL TIME:	SERVES:
30 MINUTES (PLUS OVERNIGHT COOLING TIME)	NONE	30 MINUTES	8–10

1. Combine the freshly brewed espresso, 3 tablespoons granulated sugar, and 2 tablespoons Kahlúa in a small bowl. Set aside to cool.
2. Add the eggs, egg yolk, and the remaining 3 tablespoons granulated sugar to a large mixing bowl, and beat with a mixer on medium speed until light and creamy, 4 to 5 minutes.
3. Slowly add the mascarpone, and mix until smooth.
4. Add the remaining 3 tablespoons Kahlúa, and mix again to combine.
5. Add the heavy cream and confectioners' sugar to a separate large mixing bowl, and beat with the mixer on medium speed for 2 minutes and then on high speed for another 2 minutes or until stiff peaks form.
6. Gently fold the whipped cream into the mascarpone mixture. Set aside.
7. One by one, dip the ladyfingers into the cooled espresso mixture, ensuring that they soak up the flavors but do not become too soggy.
8. Add a layer of soaked ladyfingers to the bottom of the baking dish. Spread half of the mascarpone mixture evenly over the ladyfingers. Add another layer of soaked ladyfingers, followed by the remaining mascarpone mixture.
9. Using a sifter, dust the top generously with dark chocolate cocoa powder.
10. Cover with foil and refrigerate overnight to allow the flavors to develop.
11. Slice into squares and serve cold. Store leftovers in the refrigerator for up to 3 days.

Strawberries
with Homemade Panna

This is one of the easiest and most delicious desserts you can find in many Italian American households. Sweet, juicy strawberries paired with freshly whipped panna (whipped cream) make for a light and refreshing treat. It's a dessert I love to make when strawberries are in season, and it always brings back memories of warm summer nights spent with family.

Prep Time:	Cook Time:	Total Time:	Serves:
10 minutes	None	10 minutes	4

Equipment

Knife
Cutting board
2 medium mixing bowls
Mixer or whisk
Small bowls or glasses

Ingredients

- 2 cups fresh strawberries, hulled and sliced
- 2 tbsp granulated sugar
- 1 cup heavy cream
- 2 tbsp confectioners' sugar
- ½ tsp vanilla extract

1. Toss the sliced strawberries with the granulated sugar in a medium mixing bowl. Let the strawberries sit for about 5 minutes to release their natural juices.
2. Add the heavy cream, confectioners' sugar, and vanilla extract to a separate medium mixing bowl. Using a mixer or whisk, whip until soft peaks form, about 3 to 4 minutes.
3. Serve the strawberries in small bowls or glasses, and top generously with the freshly whipped panna.
4. Enjoy immediately, or let sit for a few minutes to allow the flavors to meld together. Whipped panna is best enjoyed fresh, but leftovers can be stored in separate airtight containers in the refrigerator for up to 1 day. Rewhip lightly before serving if needed.

ZEPPOLE

Zeppole are a classic Italian treat—crispy on the outside, soft and airy on the inside, and dusted with just the right amount of confectioners' sugar. These little fried dough delights are perfect for holidays, family gatherings, or whenever you want something sweet and comforting.

PREP TIME:	COOK TIME:	TOTAL TIME:	SERVES:
10 MINUTES (PLUS 1 HOUR RESTING TIME)	20 MINUTES	30 MINUTES	6–8

EQUIPMENT

Large mixing bowl
Wooden spoon
Kitchen towel
Deep-frying pan
Slotted spoon
Paper towels
Plate

INGREDIENTS

2 cups all-purpose flour
0.25 oz (7g) packet active dry yeast, or 2¼ tsp active dry yeast
½ tsp salt
¾ cup warm water
¼ cup warm whole milk
Vegetable oil
Confectioners' sugar, for dusting

1. Combine the flour, yeast, and salt in a large mixing bowl.
2. Add the warm water and warm milk, and mix well until a smooth, sticky dough forms.
3. Cover the bowl with a clean kitchen towel, and let the dough rest for 1 hour.
4. Heat about 2 inches (5cm) vegetable oil in a deep-frying pan over medium heat to 375°F (190°C).
5. Using a spoon and your finger, and working in batches, carefully drop small dollops of the dough into the hot oil. Constantly flip the zeppole as they cook, ensuring they turn golden brown on all sides, about 2 to 3 minutes. Using a slotted spoon, transfer the zeppole to a paper towel–lined plate to drain the excess oil.
6. Generously dust the zeppole with confectioners' sugar while still warm.
7. Serve hot and enjoy! Zeppole are best enjoyed fresh, but leftovers can be stored in an airtight container at room temperature for up to 1 day. Reheat in the oven 375°F (190°C) for 7 minutes.

Ricotta Cheesecake

I've been making this ricotta cheesecake for more than 50 years. Some of my fondest memories are of standing in the kitchen late at night with my sister and sisters-in-law, rolling out dough and preparing this dessert together after long days of work. (My mother used to roll out the dough with a wine bottle because we didn't have a rolling pin back then!) It's a dessert that carries so much history, and to this day, it remains one of my favorites to make. I would suggest making this the day before serving since it requires about eight hours in the refrigerator to set. The lattice top is optional but adds a beautiful touch to this wonderful dessert.

Prep time:	Cook time:	Total time:	Serves:
20 minutes (plus 30 minutes chilling time and 8 hours resting time)	1 hour to 1 hour, 15 minutes (plus about 2 hours cooling time)	11 hours, 35 minutes	8–10

Equipment

Food processor
Plastic wrap
9-inch (23cm) springform pan
Parchment paper
Rolling pin (or wine bottle!)
Microplane or zester
Hand mixer
Large mixing bowl
Wooden spoon or spatula
Baking sheet
Knife
Scissors
Pastry brush

Ingredients

For the crust

- 1½ cups all-purpose flour
- ⅓ cup confectioners' sugar
- Pinch of salt
- 1½ sticks cold salted butter, cubed
- 2 large egg yolks, plus 1 extra for egg wash (if adding lattice top)
- 2 to 3 tbsp iced water

For the filling

- 1 (24 oz /680g) container full-cream ricotta, room temperature
- 1 (16 oz/453g) container mascarpone cheese, room temperature
- 1 (8 oz/226g) block cream cheese, room temperature
- 1½ cups granulated sugar
- ¼ cup whipping cream, room temperature
- 2 tbsp finely grated orange or lemon zest
- 2 tsp vanilla extract
- 4 large eggs, room temperature
- 3 tbsp all-purpose flour
- 3 tbsp cornstarch

1. To make the pastry, combine the flour, sugar, and salt in the bowl of a food processor. Process until combined.
2. Add the butter, 2 egg yolks, and water. Process, using the pulse action, until the dough just starts to come together. (Do not over process.)
3. Turn the dough out onto a lightly floured surface and quickly press together to form a disk-shape. Wrap in plastic wrap and place in the fridge for 30 minutes to firm. (This will make it easier to roll.)
4. Preheat the oven to 350°F (180°C). Grease the base and side of the springform pan. Line the base with parchment paper.
5. If you're making the lattice top, divide the dough into two pieces: use three quarters of it for the base and the remaining one quarter for the lattice. (If you're not making the lattice top, you can use all the dough for the base.)
6. Roll the larger piece of pastry on a lightly floured surface using a floured rolling pin until approximately 11 inches (28cm) in diameter. (If the pastry cracks in places, press those places back together.)
7. Carefully, fold the pastry back over the floured rolling pin and then unroll it into the prepared pan. Gently press the pastry down into the pan, pressing together any tears or breaks, until the pastry reaches about ½ inch (1.25cm) from the top of the pan. Refrigerate while you make the filling.
8. To make the filling, combine the ricotta, mascarpone, cream cheese, sugar, cream, citrus zest, vanilla, flour, and cornstarch in a large bowl. Beat with a hand mixer until well combined and smooth, scraping down the sides of the bowl occasionally. Add the eggs one at a time, waiting until each egg is combined before adding the next and again scraping down the sides of the bowl. (Take care not to overbeat the filling.) Place the pan on a baking sheet. Pour the filling into the crust.
9. If you're adding the lattice top, roll the remaining pastry piece on a lightly floured surface with a floured rolling pin to make a circle roughly ¼-inch (6mm) thick. Use a sharp knife to cut the pastry into ½-inch (1.25cm) wide strips. Arrange the strips into a lattice pattern on top of the cheesecake filling, pressing the strips into the pastry on the side of the pan. Use the extra egg yolk to brush on the pastry.

10 Bake for 1 hour to 1¼ hours or until the center is still a little wobbly but most of the outer part of the cheesecake is cooked. Turn the oven off and leave the cheesecake to cool in the oven for 1 hour with the door ajar to prevent cracks in the cheesecake. Remove the cheesecake from the oven and allow it to cool completely, about 1 hour more. Cover carefully with foil and refrigerate for 8 hours or overnight.

11 To serve, run a knife around the edge of the cheesecake and carefully loosen the springform's outer side. Cut into wedges to serve.

Affogato

Affogato is one of the simplest yet most indulgent Italian desserts. The contrast between hot, rich espresso and cold, creamy gelato makes every bite irresistible. It's perfect after a meal or as an afternoon treat when you need a little pick-me-up.

Prep Time:	Cook Time:	Total Time:	Serves:
5 minutes	None	5 minutes	2

Equipment

Ice cream scoop
Serving glasses or bowls
Espresso machine or stovetop moka pot

Ingredients

2 scoops high-quality vanilla gelato
2 shots freshly brewed espresso
Dark chocolate shavings (optional)
Cocoa powder (optional)
Crushed amaretti cookies or biscotti (optional)
2 tbsp liqueur, such as amaretto or Frangelico (optional)

1. Add 1 scoop vanilla gelato to each of two serving glasses or bowls.
2. Immediately pour one shot of freshly brewed hot espresso over each scoop of gelato.
3. Top with dark chocolate shavings, a sprinkle of cocoa powder, or crushed amaretti cookies or biscotti for extra texture (if using). For an added touch of indulgence, drizzle with a splash of amaretto or Frangelico (if using).
4. Serve immediately with a spoon. Affogato is best enjoyed immediately. There's no need for storage—just make it fresh and savor every spoonful!

The Traditional Dessert Basket

In Italian homes, dessert isn't always a big, elaborate affair. Often, after a meal, a basket of fresh and dried fruits, nuts, and a few sweet treats is placed at the center of the table for everyone to enjoy. This simple yet meaningful tradition encourages lingering at the table, sharing stories, and enjoying something light while sipping on espresso or a small glass of liqueur. It's a reminder that sometimes the simplest things are the most satisfying.

Prep Time:	Cook Time:	Total Time:	Serves:
10 minutes	None	10 minutes	6–8

Equipment

Knife
Cutting board
Large serving basket or platter
Small bowl (optional)
Nutcracker (if using whole nuts in shells)

Ingredients

- 4–6 fresh clementines, unpeeled
- 1 bunch of seedless green grapes
- 2 fresh pears or apples (any variety), sliced
- 6 fresh figs or ½ cup dried figs (if fresh figs are out of season)
- ½ cup dried apricots or prunes
- ½ cup pitted dates
- 1 cup whole walnuts in shells
- ½ cup whole almonds or hazelnuts
- ½ cup roasted chestnuts (optional)
- 3 oz (85g) dark chocolate, broken into small pieces
- Small pieces of nougat (optional)

1. Arrange the clementines, grapes, pears or apples, and figs (if fresh) in a basket or on a serving platter.
2. Place the dried figs, apricots or prunes, and dates around the fresh fruit, mixing colors and textures for a beautiful presentation.
3. Add the walnuts and almonds or hazelnuts, leaving some in their shells for guests to crack open at the table. Place the roasted chestnuts (if using) in a small bowl.
4. Scatter small pieces of dark chocolate and pieces of nougat (if using) among the fruit and nuts.
5. Place the basket in the center of the table, and let everyone help themselves. Serve with espresso, amaro, or a glass of dessert wine for the perfect finish to a meal. Store leftover fruit and nuts in separate airtight containers at room temperature for up to 3 days.

Struffoli

I remember standing shoulder to shoulder with my sister and sisters-in-law as we made this recipe, each of us working on a little part of the process—rolling, cutting, frying. We didn't care how hot the kitchen got or how long it took, and it wasn't just about the struffoli. It was about being together. The laughter, the stories, the way everyone had their own opinion on how small the dough pieces should be. In Italian culture, food has always brought the family together, and nothing shows that more than struffoli. These sweet little honey balls are a classic during the holidays, but in our house, they are a celebration of time spent with the people we love most.

Prep Time:	Cook Time:	Total Time:	Serves:
15 minutes (plus 15 minutes resting time)	30 minutes	1 hour	8–10

Equipment

Large mixing bowl
Plastic wrap or kitchen towel
Knife or bench scraper
Large skillet or deep pot
Slotted spoon
Paper towels
Plate
Large saucepan
Wooden spoon
Serving platter

Ingredients

- 3 cups all-purpose flour, plus more for dusting
- 4 large eggs
- 1 tsp vegetable oil
- 2 tbsp plus ¼ cup sugar, divided
- 1 tsp baking powder
- 2 tbsp whole milk
- 1 packet vanillina, or 1 tsp vanilla extract
- Vegetable oil, for frying
- 1 cup honey
- Colorful sprinkles, for topping

1. Add the flour to a clean work surface or a large mixing bowl in a mound, and make a well in the center.
2. Crack the eggs into the well, and add the vegetable oil, 2 tablespoons sugar, baking powder, milk, and vanillina. Using a fork or your hands, begin mixing, gradually incorporating the flour until a dough forms.
3. Knead the dough until smooth, 5 to 7 minutes. Wrap the dough in plastic wrap, or cover with a clean kitchen towel, and let rest for 15 minutes.
4. After the dough has rested, cut off a chunk and roll it into a long rope about ½ inch (1.25cm) thick. Cut the rope into pieces 1 to 1½ inches (2.5 to 3.75cm) long. Repeat with the remaining dough, dusting it with flour as needed to prevent sticking.
5. Add the vegetable oil to a large skillet or a deep pot, set over medium heat, and heat until the oil is hot but not smoking (about 350°F/180°C). Working in batches, fry the dough pieces, turning them as they cook, until golden brown on all sides, 1 or 2 minutes. Using a slotted spoon, transfer the fried dough to a paper towel–lined plate to drain.
6. Add the honey and the remaining ¼ cup sugar to a large saucepan, set over low heat, and cook until warm and runny, 2 or 3 minutes.
7. Add the fried struffoli to the pan, and gently toss to coat evenly.
8. Transfer the honey-coated struffoli to a serving platter, piling them into a mound or a ring shape. Immediately top with colorful sprinkles. Store leftovers in an airtight container at room temperature for up to 3 days. Do not refrigerate, or the honey will harden.

Acknowledgments

To my internet grandchildren—without your unwavering support, I never would have gotten the opportunity to write this book. I love you all more than you know!

To my grandson Matt—thank you for working with me every single day to create videos, run Nonna's Olive Oil, and of course, help me write this cookbook through every step of the process. During the past few years, our work together has truly given me a sense of purpose that was always missing.

To Brook Farling and the entire team at DK—thank you for giving me the chance to work with you on this book, which has truly become the cornerstone of my career. Without your passion and expertise, the final product couldn't have been this exceptional.

To Mark Iacono—thank you not only for your hard work in writing an incredible foreword, but also for being a great friend and source of inspiration.

To Christian Flamio and Garrett Bruce—thank you for capturing the cover photo and lifestyle shots. You couldn't have done a better job!

To Lovoni Walker, Daniel Showalter, and Ashley Brooks—thank you for capturing the incredible food images.

To Reese Bressler—thank you for your hard work on all things Nonna Gracie, but most importantly for your friendship. I'm proud to say I've earned myself another grandson.

To Jordan Bressler and the TSMGI family—thank you for the frequent and incredibly impactful contributions you've made throughout our journey. Your expertise and generosity with your time and resources have been endlessly helpful.

To Jay Lee—you believed in my grandson and gave him a chance when you had little reason to. Without that spark, none of this would have been possible, including this book.

To my daughter Rosalie and my son-in-law John—thank you for your constant guidance and advice throughout the journey of writing this book. Your support means the world.

To my bonus granddaughters, Jessica and AshLeigh—thank you for your help editing this book and, while I'm at it, for always ordering my crocheting supplies, too.

To "La Famiglia"—my daughters, Linda and Rosalie; my sons-in-law, Eugene and John; my brother and sister-in-law, Mike and Josephine; my grandchildren, Anthony and Laura, Johnny, Kristen and Mark, Matt and Jess, and Joe and AshLeigh; my sister-in-law, Anna; my brother-in-law, Joe; and my nieces and nephews, Frankie, Phyllis, Gracie, Anthony, Antoinette, and Annamaria—thank you for always cheering me on behind the scenes. Your love and support have been a constant source of strength.

To my great-grandchildren—Julia, Olivia, Matthew, and all of my great grandchildren to come—thank you for keeping me young. I hope this book serves as a North Star when you start to host your own Sunday dinners.

To the LaPietra Family—my great friends who have become chosen family since I was in my forties. I love you guys!

To Joe and Ann Raniolo—I'm thankful to God for giving me cousins who are as kind and supportive as you two.

To the Cutaia Family—Some of my most caring, genuine, and giving friends, who also run Fleetwood Bakery in Westchester, NY (highly recommend).

To Mariarosaria Perroti—my first friend in America, who went so far out of her way to help me assimilate to this new country when I was just a young girl. Your kindness has never been forgotten.

To Ann Rinaldi—thank you for your constant help and support in my day-to-day life. You've always been there for me.

To Jane Bassano—thank you for your friendship and constant encouragement. Your support has meant more than words can say.

To Susie Embich—thank you for being a great friend, especially during one of the most difficult times in my life.

To those no longer with us:

To my husband, John—although this book is dedicated to you, I love and miss you every day.

To my mom, Filomena, and my dad, Francesco—thank you for always loving and caring for me and my siblings, and for giving us the shot at the American dream. I carry your love with me every day.

To my brother, Tony, and my sister, Antoinette—thank you for being there for me and sticking by my side through thick and thin, from the very beginning until we lost you. I miss you every day.

To Loretta and Angelo LaPietra—thank you for being some of the best lifelong friends I could have ever asked for. Your friendship meant everything to me.

To Louie LaPietra—thank you for being a constant shining light in my life, with the greatest sense of humor I've ever known.

To Terry Belizzi—thank you for helping me get my first job in America and for becoming one of my dearest friends until the end. I will always cherish the time we had together.

Index

A

B

S

T

V

W

Grace Geramita, best known as "Nonna Gracie," is the internet's Italian grandma. She's known for sharing treasured Italian recipes, family stories, and kitchen wisdom with her millions of internet "grandchildren." With her warm personality, quick wit, and knack for turning simple ingredients into unforgettable meals, Nonna has become a cherished figure in households far beyond her own. Alongside her grandson, Matt Gresia, she has built a global community that celebrates food, family, and tradition. Nonna is also the founder of Nonna's Olive Oil. Born and raised in Sarno, Italy, she learned to cook at her mother's side and has been passing down those recipes ever since. When she's not in front of the camera, Nonna enjoys tending to her garden, crocheting, spoiling her grandchildren and great-grandchildren, and hosting big Sunday dinners where everyone leaves with a full belly and a smile.